Oil

A Beginner's Guide

ONEWORLD BEGINNER'S GUIDES combine an original, inventive, and engaging approach with expert analysis on subjects ranging from art and history to religion and politics, and everything in between. Innovative and affordable, books in the series are perfect for anyone curious about the way the world works and the big ideas of our time.

Oil
A Beginner's Guide

Vaclav Smil

ONEWORLD

OXFORD

A Oneworld Book

Published by Oneworld Publications 2008

Copyright © Vaclav Smil 2008

All rights reserved
Copyright under Berne Convention
A CIP record for this title is available
from the British Library

ISBN 978-1-85168-571-4

Typeset by Jayvee, Trivandrum, India
Cover design by Two Associates
Printed and bound in Great Britain by Biddles Ltd

Oneworld Publications
185 Banbury Road
Oxford OX2 7AR
England
www.oneworld-publications.com

Learn more about Oneworld. Join our mailing list to
find out about our latest titles and special offers at:

www.oneworld-publications.com

Contents

Figures

Preface

Like the other books in this series (including my previous book on energy), this is not a guide for the beginner in the strictest sense. In this particular case a certain amount of basic scientific understanding (above all reasonable numeracy) is essential. The minimum entry-level for this book could be specified as an equivalent of the North American high school education; a year or two of university studies (no matter in what subject) would make for an easier read – but, as always, it is not formal qualifications but individual interest, inquisitiveness and willingness to learn that matter most. From that point of view readers who could profit from this book range from true beginners to people who know a great deal about a specific segment of the vast oil-centered enterprise but who would like to learn more about other aspects of this inherently interdisciplinary subject of scientific inquiry.

The book teems with numbers (I am sure too many for some tastes) but I make no apologies for this: real understanding of oil's origins, geology, exploration, extraction, transportation, processing, use and linkages to society and the environment can come only by appreciating the magnitudes of specific time spans, depths, volumes, durations, rates, cumulative totals, concentrations, prices, subsidies and costs that define and govern this vast global endeavor. As for the multitude of technical terms, I have tried to explain them (however briefly) whenever they are first used. All units and their abbreviations are listed in appendix A, and appendix B offers a dozen books for additional reading and a small selection of highly informative websites.

This is my twenty-fifth book, and writing it was enjoyable, but not particularly easy: for every interesting bit of information, for every number and for every conclusion that I have included I had to leave out several times the number of fascinating facts, explanations and useful asides pointing in unexpected directions. Squeezing the universe of oil into 60,000 words of text was an unending exercise in truncation and exclusion. And although this does not excuse all omissions and imperfections of the book, I ask both the experts (who might be incensed by the absence of matters they would have considered essential) and the true beginners (who would have wished for more extensive explanations) to keep in mind the fundamental restriction under which I had to labor. Finally, my thanks to Marsha Filion for giving me another opportunity to write (within the word count bounds) without any bounds, and to Douglas Fast for preparing another crisp set of appropriate images.

World of oil

If history is seen as a sequence of progressively more remarkable energy conversions then oil, or more accurately a range of liquids produced from it, has earned an incomparable place in human evolution. Conversions of these liquids in internal combustion engines have expanded human horizons through new, and more affordable, means of personal and mass transportation. Anybody with a car in a country with decent highways can travel more than 1,000 km in the course of one day (in Europe this could entail driving in four countries). Any city with a runway long enough to accommodate large jets can now be reached from any other city on the Earth in less than twenty hours of flying time, and trips to Bali or Mauritius are no more exotic than those to Birmingham or Munich. Liquid fuels have created new landscapes of concrete and asphalt highways, overpasses, parking lots, shopping megacenters and endless urban sprawl.

Private cars also provide unprecedented access to choice. They make it easy to buy imported foodstuffs in a store at the other end of a town or to drive, on the spur of the moment, to a restaurant, symphony concert or a football game. They make it possible to live far away from a place of work, to set one's own schedule during vacation drives, to spend free time far from home by fishing or inside a garage installing monster engines and wheels or minutely reconstructing vintage car models.

Liquid fuels, through the combination of fast ships and massive eighteen-wheeler trucks, have brought us Chilean apricots and South African grapes in January and garlic and ginger from China and the Philippines all year round. Liquid fuels have also helped to rationalize productive processes ranging from farming to retailing, changes that include such remarkable organizational feats as just-in-time delivery of goods (large assembly plants working without expensive part inventories) and such profound macroeconomic changes as the runaway globalization of manufacturing where everything seems to be made twelve time zones away.

Modern life now begins and ends amidst the plethora of plastics whose synthesis began with feedstocks derived from oil – because hospitals teem with them. Surgical gloves, flexible tubing, catheters, IV containers, sterile packaging, trays, basins, bed pans and rails, thermal blankets and lab ware: naturally, you are not aware of these surroundings when a few hours or a few days old, but most of us will become all too painfully aware of them six, seven or eight decades later. And that recital was limited only to common hospital items made of polyvinylchloride: countless other items fashioned from a huge variety of plastics are in our cars, aeroplanes, trains, homes, offices and factories.

But if the new oil-derived world has been quasi-miraculous, enchanting and full of unprecedented opportunities, it has been also one of dubious deals, nasty power plays, endless violence, economic inequalities and environmental destruction. Ever since its beginnings, the high stakes of the oil business have attracted shady business deals (from J.D. Rockefeller's Standard Oil to Mikhail Khodorkovsky's Yukos) and begat some questionable alliances (be it the US and Saudi Arabia or China and Sudan). Oil ownership and the riches it provides have empowered dictators (from Muammar al-Qaddāfī to Saddām Husain), emboldened autocrats (Vladimir Putin and Hugo Chavez being only the latest prominent examples), financed terrorists (including much of *al-qāida*'s murderous activities), encouraged massive corruption (be it in Nigeria or Indonesia), promoted ostentatiously excessive consumption (mastered by the legions of Saudi princes as well as by new Russian oligarchs), engendered enormous income inequalities and done little for personal freedoms and the status of women.

Many (perhaps too many) books about oil have looked at these economic, social and political linkages. I will begin by briefly examining oil in this context before going on to explore the innumerable quotidian tasks of discovering, producing, transporting, refining and marketing the requisite volume of oil, a mass that now amounts to 4 billion tons a year. Once appreciated, these actions are no less fascinating than the world of political oil intrigues, and only their cumulatively immense ingenuity has made crude oil the single most important source of primary energy in our world.

1

Oil's benefits and burdens

Dominant energies and associated prime movers have left deep, and specific, imprints on society. The age of wood relied on low-density biomass fuels that were not always actually renewable as demand for heating and metal smelting led to often extensive deforestation and overuse of crop residues. Small mechanical prime movers powered by water and wind had a marginal role as human and animal muscles energized most tasks. The coal age introduced fuels that were more energy dense than wood, were available in a highly concentrated manner and in prodigious amounts from a relatively small number of mines, and could economically energize steam engines. These were the first inexpensive mechanical prime movers that not only replaced many stationary tasks that had previously been done by animate power, but also turned old dreams of rapid land and ocean travel into an inexpensive reality.

The introduction and diffusion of refined oil products marked an even more important qualitative shift in modern energy consumption. New fuels were superior to coal in every respect: they had higher heat content, were easier and safer to produce, cleaner and more convenient to burn and offered an incomparable flexibility of final use.

Crude oil, or more accurately a variety of refined oil products, has changed the very tempo of modern life. By allowing the introduction of more efficient prime movers they increased the productivity of modern economies and they accelerated, as well as deepened, the process of economic globalization. Their extraction and sales have fundamentally changed the economic fortunes of many countries, and they have also improved some aspects of environmental quality and added immensely to private and public comfort. The nominal price paid for these benefits – the cost of finding crude oil, extracting it, refining it and bringing the products to the market – has been, so far, surprisingly low.

The history of the oil business and of the price for crude oil paid by consumers are matters of rich documentary and statistical record and I will briefly recount some of their major events, shifts and trends. But the prices that countries and companies pay for importing crude oil and the prices consumers pay when buying refined oil products (directly as automotive fuels and lubricants, indirectly as fuels for public and freight transport and for energy embedded in the production of virtually anything sold today) tell us little about the cost of finding and producing oil, and they are obviously very different from the real cost that modern societies have paid for oil in terms of (what economists so coyly call) the externalities of its extraction, transportation, processing and combustion, as well for ensuring the security of its supply.

That is why in the closing section of this chapter I will describe some of the broader costs of oil's benefits: the environmental consequences of energizing modern economies with liquid fuels ranging from marine oil pollution to photochemical smog and to the combustion of refined products as major contributors of anthropogenic greenhouse gases; the economic, political and social impacts of both owning, and so frequently mismanaging, rich oil resources on the one hand and of being forced to buy them at what often amounts to extortionate prices on the other; and the political, military and strategic designs, calculations and decisions aimed at securing a steady flow of crude oil from the major producing regions and the wider repercussions of these activities.

What we have accomplished with oil

The beginnings of the oil era were not all that revolutionary: they started with a single product limited to just one major market as kerosene refined from crude oil became a major illuminant during the late 1860s and the 1870s. But it was not the only source of light, as city gas, made from coal, had been making great inroads in urban areas and soon afterwards both kerosene and gas were displaced by electricity. And neither the lightest nor the heaviest liquid fractions of crude oil were of much use in the early decades of the oil industry: gasoline was an inconvenient by-product of kerosene refining, too volatile and too flammable to be used for household lighting or heating, and there were no suitable small furnaces that could burn heavy oil for space heating. At least oil-derived lubricants offered cheaper and better alternatives to natural oils and waxes.

Only the invention of the internal combustion engines (gasoline ones during the 1880s and the diesel engine during the 1890s) made oil's lighter fractions potentially valuable but they became indispensable only two decades later, and then only in North America, with the emergence of large-scale car owner-ship and the diffusion of trucking (elsewhere the conversion from railroad to highway transport and the rise of car ownership began only after WWII). Less than two decades after the first motorized vehicles came the use of gasoline-powered recipro-cating engines in flight and, within a generation after this funda-mental breakthrough, the emergence of commercial aviation after WWI. During the 1950s this new business was revolution-ized by the introduction of the gas turbine, a superior internal combustion engine.

Refined fuels powering massive diesel engines also changed both freight and passenger waterborne transport: all ships that were previously fuelled by coal, from river barges to trans-oceanic liners, and from fishing vessels to large container ships (whose introduction made marine shipping a key tool of globalization) have benefited from the cleaner, cheaper, faster, more powerful and more reliable manner of propulsion. Small gasoline-powered outboard engines created a new leisure activity in motorized boating. Freight and passenger trains benefited from diesel engines, as did numerous heavy-duty construction and off-road vehicles.

Obviously, refined oil products have had their most far-reaching impact in transportation and I will note the key technical milestones of these advances and describe the current fuel requirements of these activities. The automobile was a European invention and its beginnings go back to 1876 when Nikolaus Otto (see figure 1) built the first four-stroke cycle engine running on coal gas. The first light, high-speed, gasoline-powered, single-cylinder vertical engine using Otto's four-stroke cycle was designed by Gottlieb Daimler and Wilhelm Maybach in 1885 and in the same year Karl Benz built the world's first motorized carriage powered by his slower horizontal gasoline engine. After a complete redesign by Emile Levassor in 1891 the standard car design was virtually complete by the mid-1890s: the combination of four-stroke gasoline fuelled engine, electrical ignition and a carburettor launched the largest manufacturing industry in history whose expansion still continues.

An entirely different mode of fuel ignition was patented by Rudolf Diesel in 1892 (see figure 1). Fuel injected into the cylinder of diesel engines is ignited spontaneously by high temperatures generated by compression ratios between 14–24, a range twice as high as that of Otto's engines. Diesel engines work at a higher pressure and lower speed and are inherently more efficient: their best performance can surpass 40%, compared to just over 30% for the best Otto engines. Perhaps the second most important advantage is that diesel fuel is also cheaper than gasoline yet it is not dangerously flammable. Low

Figure 1 Creators of the automobile age (clockwise): Nicolaus Otto, Karl Benz, Gottlieb Daimler and Rudolf Diesel.

flammability makes diesel engines particularly suitable in any setting where a fire could be an instant disaster (such as onboard ships) as well as in the tropics where high temperatures will cause little evaporation from vehicle and ship tanks. And the combination of high engine efficiency and low fuel volatility mean that diesel-powered vehicles can go farther without refuelling than equally sized gasoline engines. Additional mechanical advantages include the diesel engine's high torque, its resistance to stalling when the speed drops, and its inherent ruggedness.

But early diesel engines were simply too heavy to be used in automobiles and gasoline-fuelled machines were not an instant success either: for more than a decade after Levassor's redesign (and also after Charles Duryea built the first American gasoline-fuelled car in 1892) cars remained expensive, unreliable machines bought by small numbers of privileged experimenters. This changed only with Henry Ford's introduction of the affordable and reliable Model T in 1908 and with the expansion and perfection of mass production techniques after WWI. Greater affordability combined with higher disposable incomes alongside technical advances in car design and better automotive fuels led to an inexorable rise in car use, first in the US, and then after 1950 in Europe and Japan, and now throughout much of continental Asia.

The combination of America's affluence and perfected mass production gave the country a more than 90% share of the world's automotive fleet during the late 1930s, but the post-WWII economic recovery in Europe and Japan began to lower this share. In 1960, the US still had 60% of the world's passenger cars, but by 1983 Europe matched the US total and the continent is now the world's largest market for new vehicles while China became the fastest growing new car market during the 1990s. In 2005 passenger car registrations surpassed 700 million (see figure 2) and there were also more than 200 million trucks, buses and cars in commercial fleets. Because the typical performance of their engines remains rather inefficient their claim on refined fuels remains high.

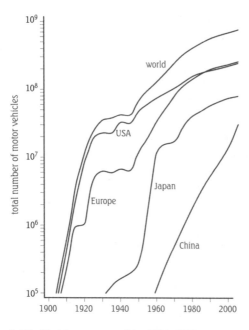

Figure 2 Worldwide car ownership, 1900–2005.

Any brief recital of the key economic, social and behavioral impacts of global car use must include, on the positive side of the ledger, unprecedented freedom of travel, expansion of individual horizons, flexibility and convenience and the enormous contribution to the prosperity of modern economies where car building is the single largest industry (in terms of added value) and where activities associated with the ownership and driving of cars create a large share of gross domestic product. The two lead items on the negative side are a large death and injury toll (worldwide, about 1.2 million deaths every year, and some twenty million injuries to drivers, passengers and pedestrians) and various environmental impacts. Traffic jams, now nearly

GASOLINE CONSUMPTION BY CARS

The best practical efficiency of the four-stroke Otto cycle engine used in gasoline-fuelled passenger cars is around 32%, but engines in everyday use commonly achieve no more than 25%. Frictional losses cut the overall efficiency by about 20%, partial load factors (inevitable during the urban driving that makes up most car travel time) reduce this by another 25%; accessory loss and (increasingly common) automatic transmission may nearly halve the remaining total so that the effective efficiency can be as low as 7–8%. Besides, for most of their history cars have not been designed to minimize gasoline consumption, and this has been particularly the case in the world's most important car market: America's preference for large cars, decades of low gasoline prices and heavy Detroit designs resulted in declining performance of the post-WWII US car fleet.

In 1974 specific gasoline consumption (expressed in Europe in L/100 km) actually increased by about 15% in comparison with the machines from the 1930s; the US uses a reverse measure of performance, miles per gallon (mpg), and hence this rate declined between the mid-1930s and 1974. Only OPEC's oil price increases brought a rapid turnaround as new federal rules (known as CAFE, Corporate Automotive Fuel Efficiency) specified gradually improving performance: the average was doubled in just twelve years, from 13.5 mpg in 1974 to 27.5 mpg (8.6 L/100 km) by 1985. Expanding imports of more efficient European and Japanese cars further improved the overall performance. Unfortunately, the collapse of high oil prices in 1985 and then the economic vigor of the 1990s reversed this trend, as pick-ups, vans and SUVs (sport utility vehicles: a monumental misnomer), all used primarily as passenger cars yet all exempt from CAFE standards, gained nearly half of the US car market and dragged average fleet efficiency backwards.

Specific performance of these excessively large and powerful vehicles is mostly below 20 mpg (above 11.8 L/100 km), some of them weigh more than 4 t and need at least 15 L/100 km in

GASOLINE CONSUMPTION BY CARS (*cont.*)

highway driving (in 2005 GMC's Yukon and Chevrolet's Suburban and Tahoe were in this monster category). Moreover, the declining efficiency has been accompanied by a steady increase in average distance travelled per year: that rate barely moved between 1950 and 1975 (up by just 3% to 15,400 km/vehicle) but by 2005 it rose by more than a quarter to reach nearly 20,000 km. High gasoline prices in 2005 and 2006 led to a weak SUV market but one should never underestimate the addiction of American drivers to these monster machines.

Better alternatives are readily available: the bestselling Honda Accord needs less than 6.5 L/100 km, the Honda Civic 5.7 L/100 km, and the hybrid Honda Insight just 3.3 L/100 km on a highway. The resumption of the 1973–1985 CAFE rate of improvement would have American cars averaging 40 mpg by 2015 and a more aggressive adoption of hybrids could bring the rate to 50 mpg (4.7 L/100 km), halving current motor gasoline consumption and sending global oil prices into retreat.

In 2005 gasoline accounted for about 25% of global refinery output, a total of roughly 900 Mt. The US share of global gasoline consumption was about 43% of the total: the country now consumes more gasoline than the combined total for the EU, Japan, China and India. The EU, with a population about 50% larger than the US and with car ownership nearly as high as in the US, consumed only about 13% of the world's gasoline. The key factors explaining this difference are a higher number of diesel engines, smaller and more efficient gasoline-fuelled vehicles, and average annual distance travelled by car being only about half of the US mean. Japan consumed 5% of all gasoline, China nearly as much (for a population ten times larger than that of Japan) and India claimed just 1%. These comparisons indicate the enormous potential demand for motor gasoline as car ownership increases in Asia's two most populous economies. They also make it clear that only a radical redesign of cars will be able to satisfy these enormous markets.

chronic in most large urban areas, loss of land (often prime farmland) to highways and parking lots and the destruction of traditional urban patterns are other common negatives.

The diesel engine has changed the world no less than its lighter but less efficient gasoline-powered counterpart. High weight/power ratio had delayed the use of diesels in passenger cars until after WWII but by the 1930s they were well on their way to dominate all applications where their higher mass made little difference, that is in shipping, on railways, in freight road transport and in agriculture.

Just before WWII one out of every four cargo ships was powered by diesel engines. Conversion to diesel accelerated after 1950 and today about nine out of ten freight ships are propelled by them, including the world's largest crude oil tankers and container vessels whose incessant traffic is the principal link between the producers and markets of the global manufacturing economy. The largest ships now have capacities in excess of 100,000 dwt and are able to carry more than 6,000 stacked containers at speeds approaching 50 km/h. Germany's Maschinenfabrik Augsburg-Nürenberg (MAN), Japan's Mitsui and South Korea's Hyundai are the leading producers of large marine diesels whose power continues to increase.

Combustion of diesel oil has multiplied the energy efficiency of railway transport as the replacement of coal-fired steam locomotives by diesel engines boosted the typical conversion efficiency from less than 10% to at least 35%. Trunk rail lines everywhere are now either electrified or use diesel-powered traction.

Diesels began to replace gasoline-fuelled vehicles in heavy road transport in 1924 when the first direct-injection diesel engine was made and when MAN and Benz and Daimler (two years before their merger) began to make diesel-powered trucks. By the late 1930s most of the new trucks and buses built in Europe were powered by diesel engines and after WWII this dominance was extended to every continent. Diesels also power most of the heavy duty machines used in construction and surface mining, a variety of off road vehicles (including trucks used in seismic exploration for oil), as well as those quintessential machines of modern land warfare, main battle tanks (although the US Abrams M1/A1 is powered by a gas turbine).

In 1926 Daimler Benz began to develop a diesel engine for passenger cars; their first model, a heavy saloon car introduced in 1936, became a favorite taxicab. Lighter, and also less polluting diesel engines were developed after 1950: consequently, the diesel engines in today's passenger cars are only slightly heavier than their gasoline-fuelled counterparts and they meet strict air quality standards. Although passenger diesels are still rare in North America, in Western Europe (with more expensive gasoline) they now have about 45% of the new car market.

A light gasoline-powered four-cylinder internal combustion engine built by the Wright brothers also powered the first flights of a heavier-than-air machine that took place at Kill Devil Hills, North Carolina on 17 December 1903 after Wilbur and Orville solved the key challenges of balance and control and proper wing design by building a series of experimental gliders. Military planes powered by high-performance reciprocating engines saw plenty of action during the closing years of WWI and commercial flight began during the early 1920s, less than two decades after the Wrights' pioneering lift-off, and by the late 1930s multi-motor hydroplanes were crossing the Pacific in stages. The performance of reciprocating aviation engines continued to improve until the late 1940s but their limits were clear: they had relatively high weight/power ratios, their reciprocating motion subjected the aeroplanes to constant vibration, they could not develop speeds in excess of 600 km/h and could not sustain flight at high altitudes, above the often violent weather.

Prospects for long-distance commercial aviation changed fundamentally with the invention of jet engines and with their rapid adoption by airlines. Although the adjective is misleading, because the machines can burn both liquid and gaseous fuels, the proper technical name for jet engines is gas turbines. They are, much like the engines that power land vehicles, trains and ships, internal combustion engines but they differ from Otto and diesel engines in three fundamental ways. In jet engines the compression of air precedes the addition of fuel in a combustor, the combustion goes on continuously rather than intermittently, and the energy of the hot air flow is extracted by a turbine that is connected to the compressor by a shaft. Gas turbines first compress the air (20–35 times above the atmospheric level) and raise its temperature (to more than 500°C) before forcing it through the combustion chamber where its temperature more than doubles. Part of the energy of the hot gas rotates the turbine and the rest generates forward thrust by exiting through the exhaust nozzle.

Specific kerosene consumption (usually measured per passenger-kilometer) has been steadily decreasing and the new

GAS TURBINES IN FLIGHT

The actual construction of the first viable jet engine prototypes was a notable case of independent parallel invention as Frank Whittle in the UK and Hans Joachim Pabst von Ohain in Germany designed the first practical engines during the late 1930s. Von Ohain's version was first tested on 27 August 1939 in an experimental Heinkel-178 and Whittle's engine powered the experimental Gloster on 15 May 1941. Improved versions of these engines entered WWII service too late (in July 1944) to make any difference to the outcome of the war.

GAS TURBINES IN FLIGHT (*cont.*)

Most of the great innovative military jet engine designs – driven by demands for ever higher speeds, altitudes and maneuverability – originated in the US and the USSR, but the British de Havilland Comet, powered by four de Havilland Ghost engines, became the first passenger jet to enter scheduled service, between London and Johannesburg, on 5 May 1952.

At 640 km/h the Comet was twice as fast as the best commercial propeller aeroplanes but it carried only thirty-six people and its engines had a very low thrust making it prone to loss of acceleration during takeoff. But these drawbacks were not the reasons for the plane's catastrophic end. After three Comets disintegrated in the air between 1953 and 1954 all Comet flights were suspended and the fatal accidents were traced to the fatigue and subsequent rupture of the pressurized fuselage. When a completely redesigned Comet 4 began flying in October 1958 two other turbojets were in regular service, the Soviet Tupolev Tu-104 and the Boeing 707. The 707 was the first in a long line of the most successful commercial jet aircraft that includes the 737 (the bestselling jetliner in history) and the jumbo 747, the first wide-body jet (in scheduled service since January 1970). This enormous plane (maximum take-off weight of nearly 400 t) was made possible by the development of turbofan engines.

By changing the gas compression and adding extra fans ahead of the compressor, two streams of exhaust gas are created – high speed core exhaust which is enveloped by a volume of slower by-pass air, this reduces noise and produces a higher thrust. While turbojets reach their peak thrust at the very high speeds needed for fighter planes, turbofans do so at low speeds, a great advantage in making heavy planes airborne. The rapid post-1970 world-wide expansion of commercial flying would have been impossible without the very high reliability and relatively low fuel consumption of turbofans.

Boeing 787 (Dreamliner) will be about 15% more efficient than its competitors. Still, the fuel consumption on long-distance flights is high: for a trans-oceanic flight nearly 45% (about 175 t) of a Boeing 747 is kerosene and at cruising altitude (typically 10–12 km above sea level) the aircraft's four engines consume about 3.2 kg of the fuel every second. Aggregate statistics show that during the last fifty years air travel had the highest growth rate among all transportation modes. The annual total of passenger-km flown globally by scheduled airlines surpassed 40 billion in the early 1950s and after doubling (on the average) in less than every six years it reached nearly 3 trillion in the year 2000 and 3.7 trillion in 2005 (see figure 3). At the same time, worldwide

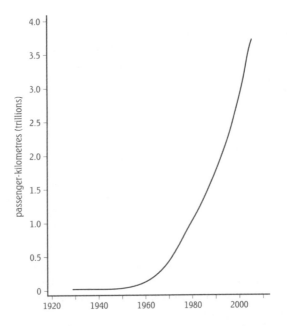

Figure 3 Exponential increase in total passenger-kilometers flown annually by scheduled airlines, 1920–2005.

air cargo services were just 200 million t-km in 1950 but by the year 2005 they were more than 140 billion t-km, nearly 90% of it on international routes. Aggregate fuel consumption in commercial aviation is less than a quarter of the total claimed by gasoline: in 2005 aviation kerosene was about 6% of total refinery output, in the US it was about 8%.

Nearly two-thirds of the world's refined products are now used in transportation (roughly 1.8 Gt in 2005) and in the US that share is now nearly 70%. The sector's dependence on liquid fuels is even higher: in the US nearly 98% of all energy used in transportation comes from crude oil, and worldwide that share is nearly 95%. Yet it can be argued that the most profound transformation effected by liquid fuels was the massive, and in affluent countries now pervasive, mechanization of agricultural tasks, a grand transformation of the most important economic activity that has been driven by a fundamental change of prime movers.

All pre-industrial agricultures (regardless of their particular organization or average productivity) were energized solely by solar radiation whose photosynthetic conversion produced food for people, feed for animals and organic wastes whose recycling replenished soil fertility. But this renewability did not translate into a reliable supply of food. Poor agronomic practices, low yields and natural catastrophes brought recurrent food shortages and higher yields required more human and animal labor.

All traditional agricultures were highly labor-intensive, commonly employing in excess of 80% of all labor. Horse-drawn machines (gang ploughs, binders, harvesters and combines) gradually began to reduce this share during the nineteenth century but the most precipitous drop came with the adoption of tractors and self-propelled agricultural machinery. US labor force in agriculture declined from nearly 40% in 1900 to less than 5% by 1970 and it is now only about 2%, and similar rates of decline have been recorded in all Western countries. The four universal measures that revolutionized traditional agriculture are the mechanization of field and crop processing tasks energized by engines and motors; the use of inorganic fertilizers, above all of synthetic nitrogen compounds; applications of agrochemicals to combat pests and weeds; and the development of new high-yielding crop varieties.

As a result, modern farming has become dependent on large-scale fossil fuel energy subsidies, most obviously in terms of liquid fuels for field, irrigation and crop processing machinery but also as energy embedded in the synthesis of agrochemicals. Productivity gains resulting from this transformation have been stunning as yields rose (tripling for many common crops during the twentieth century) and labor needs were cut. In 1900 American farmers needed an average of about three minutes labor to produce 1 kg of wheat but by the year 2000 the time was down to just two seconds and the best producers now do it in one second. The price of this progress is that, as Howard Odum aptly put it, we are now eating potatoes partially made of oil.

Agricultural mechanization was made possible above all by the use of tractors, machines first introduced in significant numbers in the US just before WWI. The power capacity of gasoline-fuelled tractors surpassed that of US draft horses before 1930, but in Europe the switch from animate to machine power took place only after WWII and it relied mostly on diesel engines that were introduced during the 1930s. Diesel engines also enabled the post-1950 shift to heavy four-wheel drive machines in the US and Canada (where the largest machines now rate about 300 kW) as well as the Soviet designs of heavy caterpillar machines. In contrast, Asia's agricultural mechanization has relied on small hand-guided two-wheel tractors (both gasoline and diesel powered) appropriate for small rice fields.

In 2005 the total number of tractors in low-income countries (just over 7 million) was only about a third of the global aggregate, while the US alone had a quarter of all tractors, and most of the most powerful ones. Diesel engines are also used in a variety of harvesting machinery, including self-propelled combines and cotton pickers. Stationary diesel engines of different sizes are also used to generate electricity, either in locations far from centralized electrical supply or in emergency situations, with the largest units as large as medium-sized steam turbines. Smaller engines are used to provide mechanical energy for refrigeration and crop processing. Given the magnitude of other final markets, agriculture (with forestry) makes a relatively small claim on refined products, amounting globally to less than 4% of the total.

Fuel oil was the first convenient substitute for solid fuels (coal and wood) whose combustion required repeated stoking and close supervision. After they bought small, automatically-fed oil furnaces millions of families, first in the US and Canada, later in Japan and Europe, could enjoy, for the first time, untended heat available at a flick of a switch or the setting of a thermostat. The worldwide switch to natural gas has reduced the number of families using fuel oil for space heating. In the US only about 8% of households (around 8 million, mostly in the Northeast) still relied on fuel oil in 2005 (compared to nearly a third in 1972), paying on the average about $0.15/L, or only about a fifth of gasoline's price. The small size of storage tanks means that delivery trucks must refill them four or even five times during a cold winter when high demand may force prices to spike. Worldwide, about 12% of all refined fuels were consumed by the residential and commercial sectors, overwhelmingly for heating.

Besides supplying the most important liquid fuels of modern civilization the process of crude oil refining is also a source of key petrochemical feedstocks that are further processed into an enormous variety of synthetic materials. Nearly 10% of all hydrocarbon liquids (roughly 350 Mt in 2005) are now used as petrochemical feedstocks, with naphtha accounting for about two-thirds of that total, followed by LPG.

PETROCHEMICAL FEEDSTOCKS AND PLASTICS

There are two major kinds of these feedstocks, olefins (mainly ethylene and propylene) and aromatics (mainly benzene, toluene and xylene). Ethylene, produced by steam cracking of ethane or naphtha, is the most important petrochemical feedstock: the EU annually produces about 20 million tons, the US more than 30 million tons. Propylene is the second most important feedstock and naphtha cracking also yields butadiene. Polymerization of basic feedstocks produces the now ubiquitous thermoplastics that account for about 80% of all man-made polymers. Thermoplastics are made up of linear or branched molecules that are softened by heating but harden again when cooled.

Polyethylene is the most important thermoplastic, most commonly encountered as a thin but strong film made into bread, garbage and grocery bags, while its common hidden uses range from insulation of electrical cables to artificial hip joints. The material is also spun into fibers and blow-molded into rigid containers for milk, detergents and motor oil, into gas tanks, pipes, toys and a multitude of industrial components.

PVC (polyvinyl chloride) is even more ubiquitous than polyethylene, found everywhere from buried pipes to credit cards, from floor tiles to surgical gloves.

Polypropylene is found in fabrics, upholstery and carpets. Propylene is also a starting material for such plastics as polycarbonates (in optical lenses, windows, rigid transparent covers and, when metallized, in CDs) and polyester resins.

Benzene is used in the synthesis of styrene (as polystyrene in packaging) and as a feedstock for a large number of other chemical reactions. Polyurethanes are a major end product of toluene and xylene is used in making polyester, solvents and films.

The second most voluminous non-fuel use of a refined petroleum product is paving with asphalt. Asphalting of roads and sidewalks began sporadically in the US during the 1870s. New York City switched from brick, granite, and wood block paving to asphalt in 1896, and all of these early pavements were made with natural asphalt from Trinidad or Venezuela. Post-WWI car use increased demand for better pavings and the growth of the refining industry supplied hot mix asphalt derived from crude oil. The American experience, expanded after WWII with the building of the interstate highways, has since been repeated in all Western nations and massive road building is now underway in China and in India.

Concrete – a mixture of cement, water and aggregates – is the most important paving material but asphalt is easier to maintain: as long as the road foundations are sound the asphalt covering can be stripped and recycled. Indeed, asphalt, not aluminum cans or newspapers, is the most massively recycled material in affluent countries. In the US about 80% of asphalt removed from worn surfaces (more than 70 million tons a year) is reclaimed and reused in new pavements. Refineries now produce nearly 120 million tons of asphalt a year, with (predictably) the US being the largest producer (about 30 million tons a year). Asphalt can also be used in roofing, industrial coatings, adhesives and in batteries.

Oil business and oil prices

In the past, multinational oil companies were seen as prime practitioners of secretive, collusive, price-fixing deals. Today, when the pricing of oil is beyond their powers, they are still seen as greedy and bloated with excessive profits. OPEC's national companies are viewed with even more distrust, subject to unending references to how they are 'having us all over a barrel'.

But it does not matter if it is Exxon and BP or OPEC, all are seen as gouging and profiteering yet at the same time, thanks to the recent panic about the imminent peak of global oil output, as unable to provide an adequate supply and hence technically and managerially inept. The realities are more complex. During the past forty years the oil business has been subject to a series of major fluctuations, with ups and downs beyond anybody's predictive powers, with troughs so deep that entire oilfields were shut down upon discovery and crests so high that surpluses and net profits broke all records.

A lack of reliable information on remaining reserves, uncertainty regarding the future revaluation of past discoveries, the impossibility of predicting sudden shifts in demand, the intervention of natural catastrophes, violent conflicts and political shifts combine to produce a market ruled by perception, fear, herd behavior, panic – and hence commonly by overreaction. One year the headlines have the world drowning in oil, a few years later they have it facing the end of the oil era. All long-range forecasts of oil prices are thus irrelevant. OPEC's *Oil Outlook to 2025*, published in 2004 just before the 2005–2006 price spike, anticipated that oil prices would settle to between \$20–25/b, proving yet again the futility of even short-term forecasts. Oil prices expressed in constant monies (adjusted for inflation) show a century long decline prior to 1970, and another period of general decline or stagnation between 1981 and 2003. The latest round of price fluctuations brought spot prices (quoted at commodity exchanges for immediate settlement) close to \$80/b in August 2006, followed by a rapid 40% decline (see figure 4), that was followed by yet another rise with daily highs above \$80/b by September 2007.

Basic facts about the global oil business involve some very large aggregates. In 2005 (assuming an average price of \$50/b) the global sales of crude oil were worth about \$1.5 trillion. This

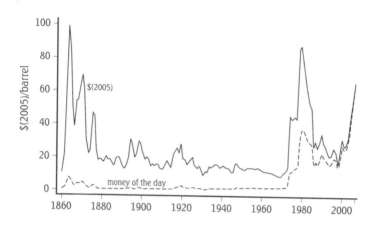

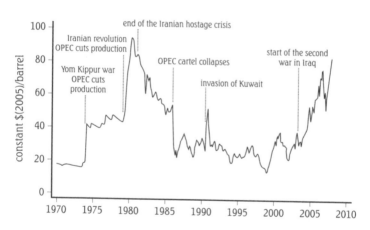

Figure 4 Crude oil prices, 1859–2007.

was equal to about 2.5% of the world's economic product of $61 trillion and a bit less than that year's GDP of Italy or Brazil; but it was only marginally more than the annual global spending on advertising, marketing and consulting services. OPEC's net oil export revenues reached about $470 billion in 2005 (and about $520 billion in 2006). Oil companies add a great deal of value by transporting and refining crude oil and by marketing the final products. Post-1973 oil price rises put the top Western oil companies ahead of car makers as the largest, and also some of the most profitable, businesses around.

In 2006, five of the world's ten largest companies were in the oil business: Exxon (number 1, with revenues of about $340 billion and profits of $36 billion), Royal Dutch Shell (3), BP (4), Chevron (6) and ConocoPhillips (10). Combined revenues of these five companies reached nearly $1.3 trillion in 2005, and as a group, the major oil companies were the most profitable US businesses in 2005 and 2006. But a longer perspective tells a less impressive story: during the last thirty years the profits of large oil companies have been highly volatile, and when compared in inflation-adjusted monies the combined annual profits of US majors remained below the 1977–1985 mean of $33 billion until the year 2000. Not surprisingly, in 1998 *The Economist* headlined the oil industry as "The decade's worst stocks." Record profits between 2004 and 2006 swiftly erased those memories from the public mind. At the same time it must be remembered that given the high taxes imposed on refined products by Western governments oil producers have actually made substantially less money than have the state treasuries.

Even in the US, where federal and state taxes on gasoline amounted to 'just' 19% of the average retail price (or to $0.58/L in 2005) the aggregate gasoline tax revenue between 1977 and 2005 was twice as large as the total profits of the major oil companies ($1.4 trillion vs. about $700 billion). In the EU and Japan, where taxes are several times the US level the government take has been much higher. And between 2000 and 2004 G7 countries collected about $1.6 trillion in taxes on liquid fuels, compared to OPEC's revenue of $1.3 trillion. Moreover, recent profits and upbeat prospects cannot change the fundamental fact that the major oil companies are in a chronic retreat that began with a wave of nationalizations during the 1970s. The global oil business is now dominated by state-owned companies and their role will only increase, as they control most of the liquid oil reserves and the areas with considerable potential for new discoveries.

NATIONAL OIL COMPANIES

These companies now control most of the world's oil reserves, and hence most of today's, and future, production. In 2005 the four largest ones – Saudi Aramco, National Iranian Oil Company (NIOC), Iraq National Oil Company (INOC) and Kuwait Petroleum Company (KPC) – held almost exactly half of all oil reserves. The next four – Pétroleos de Venezuela, Abu Dhabi National Oil Company (ADNOC), Libyan National Oil Company and Nigerian National Petroleum Company (NNPC) – controlled an additional 15%. The largest Western company, Exxon, placed twelfth (with about 1% of all reserves), behind Russia's Gazprom and Lukoil and Mexico's Pemex. Three other multinationals squeezed into the first twenty: BP at seventeenth, Chevron at nineteenth and French Total at twentieth place.

National oil companies have differed greatly in terms of their competence, performance and foresight. Norway's Statoil may be, in many ways, a model state oil company with transparent operations and extensive investment in oil exploration and production, but most of the state-run oil companies in modernizing countries have been poorly managed and perform well below their potential. The largest one, Saudi Aramco headquartered in Dhahrān on the Gulf, has been the world's largest oil producer since 1978 when it completed its compensated nationalization of Aramco's assets.

NATIONAL OIL COMPANIES (cont.)

The company has been run fairly smoothly but in a secretive manner.

Its 2005 *Facts and Figures* publication has (incongruously) a little girl in a pink dress running barefoot along a beach holding a plastic pinwheel in her raised hand – but not a single figure regarding the company's revenue (well in excess of $100 billion a year based on the sales of crude oil alone), or on its operating costs or profits. This secretiveness has led to fears that al-Ghawār, the world's largest oilfield, is nearing exhaustion and that the company will not be able to maintain a comfortably large (1.5–2 Mbpd) spare capacity, charges repeatedly denied by Aramco's management. Indeed, an aggressive expansion and investment program is now underway, aimed at raising the production capacity (oil and NGL) from 11 Mbpd in 2006 to 12 Mbpd by 2009.

The National Iranian Oil Corporation controls about 10% of global oil reserves but is managing a modern industry in a country whose laws now forbid any direct foreign equity or production concessions. NIOC can thus only award contracts that guarantee a share of eventual production from a field developed with foreign investment. Companies from Malaysia, France, Italy, Spain and China have participated in these arrangements. Output figures clearly indicate a lagging level of reservoir recovery, oilfield upgrading and modernization: in 2005 Iran produced about 4 Mbpd, 40% less than under the Shah during the mid-1970s when Iran's oil flow peaked at 6.5 Mbpd.

A free market has not been one of the hallmarks of the 150 years of oil's commercial history. The oil business has been marked by repeated efforts to fix product prices by controlling either the level of crude oil extraction or by dominating its transportation and processing, or by monopolizing all of these aspects. The first infamous, and successful, attempt to do so was the establishment of Standard Oil in Cleveland in 1870. The Rockefeller brothers (John D. and William) and their partners used secretive acquisitions and deals with railroad companies to gain the control of oil markets first in Cleveland, then in the Northeast, and eventually throughout the US. By 1904 the Standard Oil Trust (established in 1882 to manage this rapidly expanded empire, including many overseas holdings) controlled just over 90% of the country's crude oil production and 85% of all sales.

The trust was sued by the US government pursuant to the Sherman Antitrust Act of 1890 but it wasn't until 1911 that the order to dissolve it was upheld by the Supreme Court. The dissolution produced more than thirty separate companies that continued to use the Standard name and the names of the largest of these are still prominent – after repeated mergers, reorganizations, acquisitions and name changes – among the world's largest publicly traded oil companies.

Standard of New Jersey became Esso, Standard of New York (Socony) merged with Vacuum Oil Company and in 1966 it was renamed Mobil. Esso was renamed Exxon in 1972 and in 1999 it combined with Mobil to form one of several double-name oil companies, ExxonMobil. Standard Oil of California (Socal) became Chevron in 1984 and in 2001 it merged with Texaco to form ChevronTexaco (with the Texaco brand remaining only outside North America). Standard of Ohio (Sohio) was bought by BP (between 1984 and 1987) and Standard of Indiana Amoco (rebranded as Amoco in 1973) merged with BP in 1998 but the double name BPAmoco lasted only until 2000 when BP also bought Atlantic Richfield (ARCO). Atlantic and Continental Oil Company (Conoco) are two other well-known names that came out of the breakup.

This longevity of major oil companies extends beyond the Standard pedigree and beyond the US business. In the US, Gulf Oil was established in 1890, Texaco was set up in 1901, Royal

Dutch Shell was chartered in 1907, Anglo-Persian Oil Company (using the name British Petroleum since 1917) was set up in 1909. In 1928 the chairmen of Standard Oil's three largest successors, Esso, Socony and Socal and their counterparts from Royal Dutch Shell and Anglo-Persian met in Scotland's Achnacarry Castle, essentially to divide the global oil market and to stabilize the price of crude oil. After this informal oligopoly was joined by Gulf and Texaco it became widely known as the Seven Sisters (*le Sette Sorrelle*, the name used first by an Italian oilman Enrico Mattei). Their domination of the entire chain of the global oil business, from exploration to gasoline marketing, made it possible to set prices for the newly discovered oil that they began to produce after WWII in the hydrocarbon-rich countries of Asia, Africa and Latin America.

The dominance of major multinational oil companies began to weaken during the 1960s with the rise of OPEC and their global importance was rapidly reduced to a small share of their former strength by a wave of nationalizations during the 1970s. In 1960 the Seven Sisters produced more than 60% of the world's oil, by 1980 only about 28%, and by the year 2005 (for their merged descendants) it was less than 15%.

OPEC was not the first price organization set up explicitly to manage oil prices: it was modelled on the Texas Railroad Commission, a state agency that began to regulate railroads in 1891 and added responsibilities for the regulation of the oil and gas industry in 1919. After the discovery of the East Texas field brought a precipitous fall in oil prices the commission was given the right, in 1931, to control the state's oil production through prorated quotas in the form of a monthly production allowance that set the permissible percentage of maximum output. With Texas being the country's largest oil producer and the US dominating global oil output (with Texas producing more than half of the world's crude) this right amounted to a very effective cartel of worldwide importance run by an obscure state agency.

In 1950 the US still produced about 53% of the world's crude oil, a higher share than OPEC has today, but matters began to change radically during the 1950s.

Between 1950 and 1970 oil from new Middle Eastern discoveries began to reach the global market and helped to drive a worldwide economic expansion that proceeded at an unprecedented annual rate of nearly 5%. During that period US oil demand, relatively high to begin with, nearly tripled and as post-WWII Western Europe and Japan began to convert from coal to oil based economies their oil demand rose even faster so that by 1970 the affluent countries were consuming four times as much oil as they did in 1950. And the beginnings of industrialization in many low-income Asian and Latin American countries further added to the rising global oil demand. But new discoveries easily supported this rising demand and in 1960 major oil producing companies (led by the Seven Sisters) reduced their posted crude oil prices, the fictitious valuations of the extracted crude that were used for calculating the taxes and royalties owed to the oil-rich nations whose resource the majors were selling worldwide. In response to this move five oil-producing states set up the Organization of Petroleum Exporting Countries (OPEC) in Baghdad in 1960.

Saudi Arabia, Iraq, Kuwait, Iran and Venezuela were the founding members of OPEC, Qatar joined in 1961, Libya and Indonesia in 1962, Abu Dhabi in 1967, Algeria in 1969, Nigeria in 1971, Ecuador in 1973 and Gabon in 1975 (the last two countries left the group in, respectively, 1993 and 1996). Angola became the twelfth member on 1 January 2007. In order to protect their revenues the OPEC members agreed not to tolerate any further reductions of posted prices and income tax became an excise tax. By the late 1960s continuing high demand for oil began to create a seller's market. In response to this Libya increased both its posted oil price as well as the tax rate paid by the foreign oil companies in September 1971. In February 1971, twenty-two leading oil companies accepted OPEC's demand (justified by a weaker dollar) for a new 55% tax rate, an immediate increase in posted price and future price increases.

Even before this took place rising oil demand led the Texas Railroad Commission to lift its limits on production in March 1971, an epoch-ending loss of price-controlling power to the newly assertive OPEC. Concurrently, the prospect of higher oil prices began a wave of nationalizations that continued for most of the 1970s. Algeria nationalized 51% of French oil concessions in February 1971, Libya began its nationalizing with BP holdings in December 1971, Iraq took over all foreign concessions in June 1972, OPEC approved a plan for 25% government ownership of all foreign oil assets in Kuwait, Qatar, Abu Dhabi and Saudi Arabia in October 1972, and in January 1973 Iran announced that it would not renew its agreements with foreign companies when they expired in 1979. Another important change that opened the way to a new regime of global oil pricing took place in April 1973 when the US government ended the limits on the import of crude oil east of the Rocky Mountains that were set by President Eisenhower in 1959 as a fixed percentage of domestic production. This decision brought a rapid increase of US oil imports.

OPEC's new posted price of $2.59/b at the beginning of 1973 rose by 16% to $3.01 by 1 October. On 6 October Egyptian forces attacked the Israeli army along the Suez Canal, broke the Bar Lev line and advanced into Sinai; Israel eventually beat back the attack and went on an offensive deep into the Egyptian territory west of the Canal. On 16 October 1973 the six Arab Gulf states raised posted prices by 17% to $3.65/b and three days later OPEC's Arab members embargoed all oil exports to the US until Israel's pullout from occupied Arab territories (a few days later the embargo was extended to the Netherlands because Rotterdam had Europe's largest oil terminal and refineries). On 23 December 1973 the six Gulf states raised their posted price to

$11.65/b starting on 1 January 1974, a 4.5-fold rise compared to January 1973. The embargo on imports to the US was abandoned in March 1974 (it could not succeed as multinational oil companies simply rerouted their tankers) and in June Saudi Arabia raised its stake in Aramco to 60%.

OPEC's first round of steep price increases was followed by a few years of minor changes. In 1978 the price reached $12.93/b, and the Saudi government acquired complete control of Aramco and created the world's largest national oil company (in 2005 it produced about ten times as much oil as Exxon, the world's largest private operator). Effects of the quadrupling of the world oil price between 1973 and 1974 (and quintupling, in nominal terms, between 1973 and 1978) were rapid and far reaching. In North America and Europe the sudden price rise and uncertainties created by the embargo resulted initially in (a false) perception of a physical shortage of oil and led to long car queues at filling stations, fuel rationing schemes and widespread fears of being at the mercy of greedy OPEC countries in general and unpredictable oil-rich Arab regimes in particular.

These fears soon subsided (there were no physical shortages of fuels) but the serious economic consequences of the large price hike became clear as consumers and national economies, habituated to decades of low (and in real terms falling) oil prices had no choice but to pay five times as much for fuel. The full impact on the US economy (in 1974 the US imported about 22% of its crude oil demand) was delayed because of the crude oil price controls that were imposed in August 1973 during President Nixon's second term. Consequently, the average inflation-adjusted price of US gasoline in 1978 was still no higher than it was a decade earlier, and the price of refined products rose to levels unseen since WWII only after the controls were abolished on 28 January 1981 when President Reagan came into office.

Japan (with all but 0.3% of its oil imported) and most European countries (importing in excess of 90% of their oil needs) were much more vulnerable but they had one important advantage: their overall energy use was already much more efficient than in North America and the price shock only intensified these efficiency efforts and led to a higher reliance on other fuels and on nuclear electricity. Most remarkably, Japan's GDP, after falling by 0.5% in 1974, was up by 4% in 1975 even as the country's overall energy use fell by nearly 5%. OPEC's windfall was large: the total revenues of its member states tripled between 1973 and 1978 but high inflation generated by quintupled oil prices meant that between 1974 (after the initial hike) and 1978 world oil prices actually fell in real terms.

But a second round of oil price rises was just about to begin. Demonstrations against Shah Mohammed Reza Pahlavi began in Tehran in January 1978, by the end of the summer Iran was under military rule and by December its oil production fell sharply. On 16 January 1979, when the Shah fled into exile, OPEC's oil price averaged $13.62/b; twelve months later, with Ayatollah Khomeini back in Iran and with the US embassy occupied by student radicals, the price nearly doubled to $25.56/b. A year later (after Iraq invaded Iran in September) it was $32.95/b. The peak was reached in March 1981 with the average at $34.89/b, the best-quality crude oils selling on the spot market for around $50/b, and experts widely predicting prices of $100/b in just a few years.

Economies that had begun to recover from the first price hike were hit again, and more seriously. In 1982 the US GDP fell by 2%, but the record high oil prices caused the greatest setbacks in Asia, Africa and Latin America: their industries, transportation and also urban cooking (using kerosene stoves) depended on oil imports and high (and dollar denominated) prices were consuming a rising share of their export earnings. But with the second round of price rises OPEC clearly overplayed its hand. Unlike the first time around, oil prices rose high enough to do three things that greatly weakened OPEC's dominance of the market.

The resulting economic slowdown depressed the global fuel demand: by 1983 it was 10% below the 1978 peak (and in the US the cut was 21%); it reinforced the drive for higher energy efficiency; and it led to vigorous oil and gas exploration and development in non-OPEC countries. The results of this combination were impressive. In 1978 non-OPEC oil producers (excluding the USSR) extracted 35% of the world's oil but in 1983 their share rose to 45% while OPEC's share fell to just 31%.

At first OPEC tried to keep the prices high, lowering the marker rate to only $33.63 during 1982, but the oil glut persisted and by early 1983 it had to cut it to $28.74/b. The end came in August 1985 when the Saudis decided to stop acting as the swing producer (repeatedly cutting their oil output to prop up the falling prices) and linked their oil price to the spot market values and at the beginning of 1986 doubled their extraction in order to regain their lost market share. Oil prices fell to $20/b by January 1986 and in early April they dipped below $10/b before they temporarily stabilized at around $15/b. They remained low for the remainder of the 1980s and even the Iraqi invasion of Kuwait (on 2 August 1990) and the First Gulf War (16 January–28 February 1991) produced only short-lived spikes followed by a decade of prices that stayed mostly between $15–20/b.

The weighted average of all export prices reached $23/b in January 1997 but the drop in demand caused by a short but severe Asian financial crisis depressed the price to just $9.41/b by December 1998. Once again, low oil prices were being taken for granted and, once again, energy demand began rising even in those rich nations that were already by far the largest users, and importers, of oil. During the 1990s energy consumption rose by almost 15% in the USA, 17% in France, 19% in Australia and, despite a stagnating economy, 24% in Japan. As a result, OPEC's share of global oil output rose again to above 40%

and oil prices rose to more than \$25/b by the end of 1999 and briefly surpassed \$30/b in September 2000. Prices fell again with the onset of the worldwide economic recession in the wake of the terrorist attack on the USA on 11 September 2001. Prices stayed mostly between \$20–25/b during the year 2002, spiked above \$30/b in early 2003 and after a brief fall began to rise in April 2003.

THE LATEST OIL PRICE SPIKE

During the latter half of 2003 the crude oil price rose once again to the range of \$25–30/b and during 2004 came close to, and briefly above, \$40/b. The rising trend continued in 2005 and for the first eight months of 2006 until, in August 2006, the weighted mean of all traded oil peaked at \$71.45/b. Several developments combined to produce this latest round of substantial oil price rises.

Certainly the most important factor was the sudden increase in demand, both by traditionally large Western oil importers and by the rapidly expanding Chinese and Indian economies. During the first three years of the twenty-first century annual demand increments were, respectively, just 0.7, 0.6 and 0.9 Mbpd, but in 2003 the rate jumped to nearly 1.4 Mbpd, in 2004 it doubled to almost 2.8 Mbpd and in 2005 it was still 1.1 Mbpd.

But the price rise was also driven by the fear that oil supply shortages could be caused in the future by the unsettled situation in Iraq, and by concerns about terrorist attacks in general and strikes on Saudi oilfields or oil terminals in particular. Moreover, low stock market returns attracted speculative investments in oil futures, and all of this while the media were disseminating stories about an imminent peak of global oil production that was to herald the painful end of modern civilization (see chapter 5).

But, contrary to the widespread expectation of deepening supply shortages that were to bring a \$100 barrel in a matter of months, oil prices did what they have always done after a spike that had no justification in physical shortages of the fuel: they

THE LATEST OIL PRICE SPIKE

rapidly retreated from their highs. After reaching a peak in August 2006 (on 8 August OPEC's reference basket of crude oils was valued at $72.68/b) prices fell 15% within a month, another 14% by the end of October, and had dropped to $55.97/b at the end of the year. By January 11, 2007 they fell below $50/b, a third lower than the record just five months before. This price retreat reflected a weakening demand: preliminary figures showed global consumption up by only 0.8 Mbpd in 2006, that is, returning to the increments that prevailed before the anomalous jump between 2001–2003. OPEC's official outlook for 2007 was for an increase of no more than 1.25 Mbpd. Nevertheless, the average price of OPEC oil began to rise again in January 2007 and by October it surpassed $80/b, higher than in summer 2006.

Nobody is in control of oil prices – or else that entity would have a peculiar taste for wild swings and a near-permanent lack of stability (see figure 5). The key lessons from this high price volatility and the global economic consequences of these unpredictably excessive fluctuations have been widely ignored or misinterpreted. In the first place, the price gyrations in general and high post-1970 prices in particular have never reflected any imminent or rapidly approaching physical shortage of oil, as the resource remains abundant. A key reason for high price spikes has been an artificial scarcity repeatedly created by OPEC that has hardly rushed to supply the world: its production in 2004 was just 5% above the level it reached a quarter of a century ago, in 1979, but given its low production costs (less than $5/b) it has exacted enormous transfers of wealth, mostly from affluent countries but recently from such populous modernizing nations as China and India.

Unfortunately, there is little hope for any long-term stability of oil prices, and not because the world is on the verge of

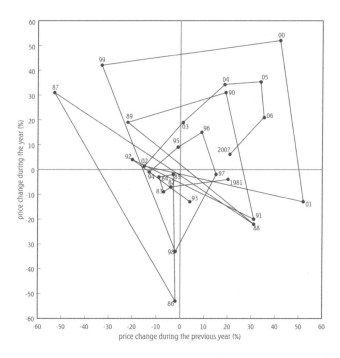

Figure 5 Year-to-year changes of oil prices, shown here for twenty-five years between 1981–2007, reveal virtually random shifts that are impossible to forecast.

drastically declining supplies of oil. The problem is that OPEC has enough clout to try to set the price but not enough control over the market to make it work beyond the short term.

The greatest challenge for OPEC is to keep the price below the level that would lead to a substantial drop in demand for oil, to increased hydrocarbon exploration in non-OPEC countries and to government-subsidized investment towards alternative energy sources. In its public pronouncements OPEC repeatedly professes its commitment to a stable oil market and security of supply, but its actions have often had the very opposite effect.

At the same time it is true that OPEC is not a sole price setter and that speculation on the three major international petroleum exchanges (in New York, London and Singapore) can exacerbate its actions, particularly during exaggerated reactions to sudden shifts (recessions, suddenly booming demand), catastrophic events (such as Hurricane Katrina that cut the Gulf of Mexico production) or to the mere fear of them (what if terrorists attack Rās Tanūra, the world's largest oil terminal?).

Oil links and the real cost of oil

The world's single most important source of fossil energy and its truly worldwide extraction, transportation, processing and combustion affect every realm of modern life. The performance of all but the poorest economies, matters of both domestic and international politics in both oil exporting and oil importing countries, quality of life, a great deal of strategic thinking on the part of major powers, particular military actions during times of war and the state of the Earth's environment – all of these are demonstrably linked to oil, but virtually all of these linkages are complex and often counterintuitive. Primary energies of fossil fuels have been the necessary engines of modern economies but their abundance alone is not enough to bring admirable economic achievements and to guarantee an improving standard of living.

Just before its demise the USSR was the world's largest producer of both crude oil and natural gas but the country's economy was a dismal underperformer and the average income of Soviet citizens was a fraction of the French or German mean although those two countries had to import virtually all of their oil. Modernizing (an adjective I prefer to developing) oil-rich nations in general, and OPEC nations in particular, provide even better examples of this reality. Except for Indonesia (223 million in 2005), Nigeria (132 million) and Iran (70 million), OPEC nations have very small or relatively small populations and since the early 1970s they have benefited (albeit, as just explained in the previous section, in a highly fluctuating manner) from enormous transfers of wealth. For example, in

OIL, HUMAN DEVELOPMENT, FREEDOM AND CORRUPTION

One of the most revealing international comparisons is the Human Development Index (HDI) that is composed of three major components: life expectancy at birth; adult literacy rate and combined gross enrolment ratio in primary to tertiary education; and GDP per capita expressed in terms of purchasing power parity dollars. This simple shortcut serves well as an indicator of a nation's relative achievements and it reveals that none of the oil-rich Middle Eastern nations is performing well. There are 177 nations listed, with a maximum score of 1.0. Norway, Iceland, Australia, Canada and Sweden top the global ranking with 0.95–0.96. However, in 2005 even tiny, super-rich Kuwait was placed at 44 worldwide, Saudi Arabia was at 77 and Iran at 99. (see figure 6).

country	HDI rank	GDP minus HDI rank	political freedom index	corruption perception	
				index	rank
Qatar	40	-13	6	6.0	32
United Arab Emerates	41	-18	6	6.2	31
Kuwait	44	-11	4	4.8	46
Oman	71	-30	6	5.4	39
Saudi Arabia	77	-33	7	3.3	70
Iran	99	-29	7	2.7	105

HDI rank among 177 ranked countries. Political freedom index: 6-7 not free; 4-5 partially free.
Corruption perception rank among 163 ranked countries.

Figure 6 Oil-rich Middle Eastern under-performers.

OIL, HUMAN DEVELOPMENT, FREEDOM
AND CORRUPTION (*cont.*)

Even more telling is the difference between the rank of the average per capita GDP of a country and its HDI rank: positive numbers identify the nations whose state of development is higher than expected when judged solely by their GDP, negative numbers apply when a nation's HDI lags behind its GDP. In this respect, all oil-rich Persian Gulf nations have been dismal underperformers: not only do they have negative scores, but these score are the highest worldwide, indicating that no other group of countries has used its riches so unwisely (see figure 6).

And while national income inequality statistics are not available either for Saudi Arabia or Kuwait, most of the oil-exporting countries have a very high Gini index, the most commonly used measure of economic inequality, with 0 signifying perfect income equality and 100 total inequality. Iran's score is roughly 45, Nigeria's and Venezuela's about 50, and Mexico's 55, in contrast, the top achievers, Japan and Norway, score 25.

Rankings by the political freedom index put five Persian Gulf oil producers (Saudi Arabia, Iran, Iraq, UAE, Qatar, Oman) as well as Libya and Algeria into the bottom, not free, category and Kuwait, Nigeria and Venezuela into the lower ranks of the partly free group. Another revealing set of comparisons concerns corruption. Transparency International's Corruption Perception Index for the year 2006 ranges from the cleanest Finland (9.6) to hopeless Haiti (1.8). Nigeria, Venezuela and Indonesia are at near-Haiti levels of, respectively, 2.2, 2.3 and 2.4. Russia joins this unenviable oil-rich group with a corruption index of 2.5. Iran rated 2.7, while Saudi Arabia and Mexico both scored 3.3 (see figure 6).

The evidence is clear: modernizing oil-rich countries in general, and the Middle Eastern nations in particular, have not used their considerable wealth to build truly more modern, more equitable and less corrupt societies with a higher quality of life. In fact, the opposite is true as they embody (to an exceptionally high degree) many negatives that prevent real modernization of their societies.

2005 Saudi Arabia had a budget surplus of $57 billion, more than $2,000/capita for every one of its citizens. However, as the just-noted international comparisons show, these fabulous earnings have not been translated into commensurate economic and social advances.

And the oil-rich countries have not done particularly well even in terms of gross economic growth: post-1960 data shows that well-managed resource-poor countries performed better (their economies growing up to two to three times faster) even after adjusting for the initial per capita income. The lagging performance of resource-rich countries became pronounced only during the 1970s, after higher oil prices boosted their revenues. Pablo Pérez Alfonso, a founder of OPEC, spoke of oil as a curse, bringing waste, corruption and excessive consumption: three decades later his conclusion has been confirmed and reconfirmed (with the exception of Norway) with every oil-price spike.

And it does not get any better once we turn to politics, stability of governments and civil institutions and long-term prospects for security. There are only two non-Western oil-rich countries (Qatar and United Arab Emirates) whose politics and stability are not matters of chronic concern and anxious speculation. Worries about long-term stability in most of OPEC's countries, and particularly in Saudi Arabia, Iran and Nigeria, have generated a vast speculative literature during the past quarter century and more warnings and catastrophic scenarios are sure to come. Perhaps the most useful fact to keep in mind is that most of these writings are produced by people who understand neither Arabic nor Farsi and whose knowledge of the culture steeped in Islam is limited to repeating such often misunderstood terms as *jihād* or *fatwa*.

Any assessment of the world's pivotal oil producer must take into account the secretive nature of decision-making within Saudi Arabia's extensive ruling family and the complexity of the country's traditions and its slowly unfolding reforms. Unfortunately, we are most often offered caricatures rather than revealing portraits of the country. Most notably, the Saudi royal family is repeatedly portrayed as unstable, insecure and out of touch and many have explicitly predicted its imminent (and violent) demise when the corrupt and incompetent princes will be swept away by religious zealots or by impatient reformers.

The analytical and interpretive task is no easier as far as Iranian affairs are concerned. Outsiders have to reckon with the complex dynamics of the now decades-long struggle for influence and power among fundamentalists, nationalist zealots (recently emboldened by rising oil earnings and the US entanglement in Iraq) and more pragmatic leaders tacitly supported by a large share of the country's young (but tightly controlled) population. The latest fashion has been to portray Iran as an almost superpower-like actor whose expansive designs for a new *shī'ī*-dominated Middle East will, at minimum, destabilize the entire region and may even lead to a global conflict.

Matters do not get any better when attention turns to the violence and extraordinary level of corruption and political tension in Africa's most populous state, Nigeria. Oil production in the Niger Delta has been repeatedly disrupted by rebels who blow up pipelines and oil terminals, and kidnap oil workers and executives, even as a chronic discord between the federal and state governments is being exacerbated by rising income inequalities and by a radicalization of the Muslim North. Some commentators see Nigeria's current problems as the precursors of an almost inevitable new civil war or protracted anarchy.

And the litany of concerns does not end with these great oil players. Algeria has been through a long and brutal civil war as the secular government fought the fundamentalists and the stability of its regime remains uncertain. And although Libya has publicly forsaken its decades of erratic and violent ways (bombing a Pan Am flight in 1988, supporting terrorist movements abroad, developing nuclear weapons) this did not change its strongman regime and it remains uncertain how far this new-found moderation will go. In Indonesia the major worry is no longer pervasive corruption but the degree to which this most populous Muslim nation will embrace a more fundamentalist form of its faith. The rest of this section could be filled with a recounting of recent concerns about Russia's authoritarian trends whose consequences have ranged from *de facto* re-nationalization of oil companies to the suppression of the independent media.

Oil's impact on politics and policies is also ever-present in affluent countries whose prosperity is underpinned by large-scale oil imports, and its expressions range from questionable attitudes toward oil-exporting nations to the use of oil imports as a reason for not just advocating but heavily subsidizing some dubious alternative energy sources. Attitudes toward oil-producing nations find their most extreme expressions as far as Middle Eastern countries are concerned. Among the Western political elites these feelings have ranged from kowtowing to unsavory rulers and eagerly selling them arms all the way to calls for the US to rethink (at minimum) its ties with what many commentators see as terrorism-breeding, fundamentalist, treacherous and family-ruled Saudi Arabia. Many politicians and activists see the best long-term solution to cutting the addiction to oil imports from the chronically unstable Middle East in developing alternative sources of liquid fuels.

During the late 1970s this led to a very expensive commitment to a massive development of oil from the Rocky Mountains oil shales (promptly aborted), and recently this quest has led to an uncritical embrace of heavily subsidized and environmentally unfriendly corn-derived ethanol. From a purely economic standpoint it is counterproductive to divert (always limited) resources to endeavors that would produce a much more expensive substitute, especially as the chances of any lasting embargo on oil exports from countries whose very survival depends on them are highly unlikely (al-Qaddāfī's Libya or Khomeini's Iran have been equally faithful suppliers of oil to the West as its supposedly great strategic ally, Saudi Arabia). But after 9/11 it is not easy to dismiss the possibility of a major production cut in a country hijacked by a Taliban-like government. Saudi Arabia turned into a medieval style caliphate might

OIL AS CASUS BELLI

Oil's strategic role has been consistently overplayed by some careless historians. The most notorious example of these exaggerated claims is that Japan attacked Pearl Harbor in 1941 because in July 1940 President Roosevelt had terminated the licenses for exports of aviation gasoline – the attack on the US was to clear the way for the assault on South-East Asia with its Sumatran and Burmese oilfields. But to see Japan's aggression as an oil-driven quest is to forget that the attack on Pearl Harbor was preceded by nearly a decade of expansive Japanese militarism with its 1933 conquest of Manchuria and 1937 attack on China, actions that had nothing to do with oil. And the quest for foreign oil was obviously not a motivating factor behind WWI or in Hitler's serial aggression that caused WWII, and it had no role in the genesis of major post-WWII conflicts involving the two superpowers (the Korean War, the French and then US war in Vietnam, the Soviet occupation of Afghanistan) or in many cross-border wars (Sino-Indian, Indo-Pakistani, Eritrean-Ethiopian and many others).

In contrast, indirect foreign interventions in Middle Eastern countries (arms sales, military training, generous economic aid) have aimed either at stabilizing or subverting governments in the oil-rich region. Their most obvious manifestation during the Cold War was the toppling of Mossadegh's government in Iran in 1953, the sales (or simply transfers) of Soviet arms to Egypt, Syria, Libya

OIL AS CASUS BELLI (*cont.*)

and Iraq and the concurrent American arms shipments to Iran (before 1979), Saudi Arabia and the Gulf states and the Western support of Iraq during its long war with Iran (1980–1988). And, of course, the Gulf War (1991) and the US invasion of Iraq in 2003 have often been portrayed as purely oil wars.

Saddam Hussain's occupation of Kuwait in August 1990 doubled Iraq's crude oil reserves (to about 20% of the world total) and it also directly threatened the nearby supergiant Saudi oilfields and hence the survival of the monarchy that controls a quarter of the world's oil reserves. The massive anti-Saddam coalition and half a million troops engaged in operation Desert Storm in 1991 could thus be seen as a perfect example of an oil-driven war. But other concerns were also at play: Hussain's quest for nuclear weapons with which the country could dominate and destabilize the entire region and the risk of another Iraqi–Iranian or Arab–Israeli war. And if the control of oil was the primary objective of the 1991 Gulf War why then were the victorious armies not ordered to occupy at least Iraq's southern oil fields?

Similarly, more complex considerations were behind the conquest of Iraq in March 2003: a decade-long refusal of the Iraqi regime to comply with numerous UN resolutions, the traumatic impact of 9/11 attacks on US foreign policy (leading to the shift from the isolation of a hostile regime in Baghdad to the pre-emption of a possible new attack). Above it all was the grand strategic objective of eventually having an elected government in a pivotal state in the Middle East that might serve as a powerful and stabilizing political example in a very unsettled region and be a mighty counterweight to any radicalizing tendencies. What many commentators see simplistically as a clear-cut case of oil-driven war has been anything but that. Besides, the cost of the first four years of Iraq's occupation, the parlous state of Iraq's oil infrastructure and the country's limited oil production added up to an enormous financial liability for the US rather than to any enviable gain, oil or otherwise.

forsake half of all oil earnings, and given the trivial sums involved in the new asymmetric warfare based on suicide bombings (bin-Lādin boasted that the World Trade Center attack cost *al-qāida* only $500,000) the anti-Western *jihād* could be financed in other ways (from émigré remittances to taxing pilgrims to Mecca).

But there is no doubt about the importance of oil for modern armies. WWI was still dominated by railways, horse-drawn carriages and forced marches, but WWII was the first largely mechanized conflict relying on massed trucks, tanks and planes. Fuel demands rose afterwards with the development of better armed and more powerful tanks and with the introduction of jet aircraft. America's 60-t M1/A1 Abrams battle tank consumes kerosene at no less than 400 L/100 km (Mercedes S600 needs 15 L/100 km and Honda Civic 8 L/100 km). Kerosene requirements of supersonic combat aircraft are so high that no extended mission can be flown without in-flight refuelling from tanker planes. Not surprisingly, the US Department of Defense has by far the highest oil consumption of all government agencies: in 2005 its demand accounted for 92% of all refined fuels bought by the government. But, again, a caveat is in order: oil supremacy is not a decisive factor in asymmetrical conflicts, a reality amply demonstrated in Vietnam, by the suicide attacks of 11 September 2001 or by the relentless suicide bombings in Baghdad.

Oil and the environment

Perhaps the most newsworthy environmental impacts of the oil industry are the periodic accidents when giant tankers spill large volumes of oil into the sea and onto beaches, resulting in long-lasting pollution of beaches or rocky shores and the highly publicized mass mortalities of sea birds. Less noticeable is the contamination of zooplankton and the persistent presence of oil in anoxic sediments that has a long-term influence on benthic invertebrates. The worst tanker accidents have been those of *Atlantic Express* that spilled 287,000 t off Tobago in 1979 and *ABT Summer* that released 260,000 t off Angola in 1991. Both of these mishaps took place far offshore and hence they received much less attention than the world's third and fourth largest record spills, *Castillo de Belver* that released 253,000 t of crude off South Africa's Saldanha Bay in 1981, and *Amoco Cadiz* much of whose cargo of 223,000 t of light crude ended up on the beaches of Brittany in 1978.

By 2006 there were also six spills greater than 100,000 t, and the studies of causes show that groundings, collisions and hull failures have been (in that order) the main reasons for these mishaps. The good news is that the frequency of both large and small spills has been constantly declining since the 1970s and that the aggregate quantity spilled annually in recent years has been well below the amount of oil reaching the sea from natural seeps. The bad news is that long-term studies of oil spill sites have shown unexpected persistence of toxic sub-surface oil and chronic sublethal exposure with lasting effects on wildlife. Much of this new understanding was gained by follow-up studies of the most notable North American tanker spill, that of *Exxon Valdez* in Alaska's Prince William Sound on 24 March 1989. The grounded ship released only 37,000 t of oil but the spill killed perhaps as many as 270,000 water birds and it left many long-lasting effects on other biota.

Exxon paid about (1990) $2 billion on oil clean-up and another billion to the state of Alaska, the costs of restoring waters and (at least superficially) the rocky shores and beaches of Prince William Sound were thus internalized to a degree unprecedented in previous oil spill accidents. In contrast, the Mexican IXTOC 1 well in Bahia de Campeche spilled perhaps as much as 1.4 Mt in 1979–1980 without any penalties being paid by Pemex. Fortunately, most of the almost routine, unreported spills of crude oil or refined products are small-scale events that do not overwhelm the natural processes of evaporation, emulsification, sinking, auto-oxidation and, most importantly, microbial oxidation, that limit their impact on surface waters or aquifers.

Most new tankers are built with double hulls, and only double-hulled ships will be allowed in EU waters by 2010 and in the US by 2015. What will not change are the flagging and crewing of oil tankers. Most of the world's tankers (and other freight vessels) fly a flag of convenience which means that their ownership and control has nothing to do with the country of registration. Such registrations, now offered by nearly 30 countries (Liberia, Taiwan, Honduras, Belize, Panama, Malta and Spain are the leading flag-of-convenience providers, but the list also includes landlocked Bolivia and Mongolia) provide cover for substandard practices and for evading legal responsibility for oil spills.

The Kuwaiti well fires of 1991 were perhaps the most prominently reported environmental catastrophe involving the combustion of crude oil. More than 700 oil and gas wells were set ablaze (it took nine months to extinguish them) and because the very small particles generated by oil combustion can stay aloft for weeks they were carried far downwind: only ten days after Iraqi troops set fire to Kuwaiti oil wells in late February 1991 soot particles from these fires were identified in Hawaii. In subsequent months solar radiation received at the ground was reduced over an area that extended from Libya to Pakistan, and from Yemen to Kazakhstan. But oil combustion has a much more important environmental, and health, effect because of its generation of the three key precursors of photochemical smog, carbon monoxide, volatile organic carbohydrates (VOC) and nitrogen oxides (NO_x).

Photochemical smog was first observed in Los Angeles in the 1940s and its origins were soon traced primarily to automotive emissions. As car use progressed around the world all major urban areas began to experience seasonal (Toronto or Paris) or near-permanent (Bangkok, Cairo) levels of smog, whose effects range from impaired health (eye irritation, lung problems) to damage to materials, crops and coniferous trees. A recent epidemiological study in California also demonstrated that the lung function of children living within 500 m of a freeway was seriously impaired and that this adverse effect (independent of overall regional air quality) could result in important deficits later in life.

Introduction of three-way catalytic converters (reducing emissions of CO, VOC and NO_x) helped to limit smog levels but their use had to be preceded by production of unleaded fuels in order to avoid the poisoning of the platinum catalyst. By that time decades of leaded gasoline consumption had created high levels of lead contamination in all urban areas with high traffic density. Lead's phase-out began in the US in 1975 and it was completed by 1990. Methyl tertiary butyl ether (MTBE, produced from isobutylene and methanol) became the most common additive to boost octane rating and to prevent engine knock, and starting in 1995 it made up as much as 15% of the reformulated gasoline designed to limit air pollution. But because MTBE is easily miscible with water and leaks had conta-minated many water wells, a switch to ethanol began in 2003 and accelerated by 2006.

Combustion of refined fuels generates less CO_2 per unit of released energy than does the combustion of coal, but in aggre-gate they became the world's largest source of carbon from burning fossil fuels in 1968 when they accounted for about 43% of the total. The share of carbon from liquid fuels rose to nearly 50% by 1974 but during the late 1980s it was basically the same as for coal combustion only to pull ahead once more during the 1990s: by 2000 liquid fuels contributed about 41% of all carbon from fossil fuel combustion. Unlike solid fuels, whose emissions now come, almost without exception, from stationary sources (potentially controllable by the sequestration of CO_2), the bulk of the carbon emissions from liquid products comes from the transportation sector and the only possible control is to prevent their generation. Combustion of every litre of gasoline releases about 2.3 kg of CO_2 and the rate for diesel fuel is 2.6 kg/L.

All of these economic, strategic, health and environmental burdens should be considered in any serious attempts at finding the real cost of oil – but these efforts are exceedingly compli-cated because of the many assumptions, approximations and uncertainties that are required to quantify externalities (What is the cost of a smog-induced asthma attack?), to answer counter-factual questions (How much would the US Department of Defense save if the Middle East contained no oil, but was still full of Muslim *jihādis* bent on attacking the US?), and to set the analytical boundaries (Should the entire cost of urban sprawl be charged to gasoline?).

Obviously, these challenges have no definite solutions and hence the estimates of the real price of crude oil or gasoline can end up with totals only somewhat higher than the prevailing price or costs that are an order of magnitude above the current price. An excellent example in the latter category is the study of the real cost of US gasoline completed by the International Center for Technology Assessment in 1998 when Americans were paying just over $1/gallon. Inclusion of tax and program subsidies to oil companies, protection (mainly military) subsidies, environmental, health and social costs (ranging from air pollu-tion to urban sprawl) and other outlays (from travel delays due to road congestion to uncompensated damages due to car accidents and subsidized parking) raised the real cost to between $5.60 and $15.14/gallon.

I am very much in favor of more realistic cost estimates but I must also note that these exercises have many methodological problems and are inherently biased as they do not consider the many benefits arising from the use of these subsidized fuels. Different assumptions and non-uniform analytical boundaries result in incompatible conclusions: do the US oil companies enjoy unconscionable subsidies or are their benefits relatively minor? Does the production and use of automobiles add up to a net benefit or a net burden in modern economies? Ubiquitous examples of unaccounted benefits range from lives saved by rapid transfers of patients to hospitals by ambulances, time saved by flying as opposed to taking trains, or better air quality compared to burning wood or coal. No single answer is possible but the key conclusion stands: prices paid for refined oil products certainly do not reflect their real cost to society.

2

What oil is and how it was formed

Most people are fairly familiar with at least one of the many economic, social and political consequences of humanity's dependence on oil that were reviewed in the first chapter. In contrast, most people know little or nothing about the intricate and complex origins of crude oil and about the actual composition of this valuable commodity that has such a central role in our lives.

The generic term 'oil' designates two very different kinds of compounds that are liquid at ambient temperature and normal atmospheric pressure. Crude oils (using the proper qualifying adjective and a plural whose importance will be explained shortly) that oil companies extract from the topmost layer of the Earth's crust belong, together with other mineral substances whose composition is dominated by hydrogen and carbon, to a class of compounds called hydrocarbons: these can be gaseous (natural gases), liquid, or solid (bitumens, tars). Oils that abound in the biosphere and that form an important part of our diet (as plant oils extracted from seeds and nuts) or enhance our drinks and perfumes (delicate essential oils in herbs or the rinds of citrus fruit) are not, despite their similar make-up, classed as hydrocarbons, while the reverse term, carbohydrates, is reserved for organic molecules whose carbon and hydrogen atoms form simple sugars (mono- and disaccharides) whose polymers yield starches and cellulose, the biosphere's most abundant organic materials.

WHAT IS IN A NAME?

Naphtha, an ancient Persian word for a dark liquid coming from the ground, was adopted in classical Greek but most European languages eventually accepted variations of the Greek rock oil, πετρέλαιο – English petroleum, French *pétrole*, Italian *petrolio* – or its literal translations, such as German *Erdöl*, Dutch *aardolie*. Because petroleum has to be processed (refined) to produce a variety of liquid fuels that are suited for specific uses, an accurate generic term for the substance, and a common American usage, is simply crude oil (German *Rohöl*, French *pétrole brut*). In modern Western usage the term naphtha has contracted to designate a specific range of refined crude oil products (see chapter 4).

The ancient Persian word was retained in its original broad meaning as the Arabic نفط (*naft*) and it also migrated into Slavic languages: Russian нефть (*neft'*), Czech *nafta*. However, modern Arabic now habitually uses the import from Greek, as newspapers write about بترول (*bitrūl*). Chinese and Japanese use the same two characters 原油 for the crude oil; their standard (*putonghua*) Chinese pronunciation is *yuán yóu* and Japanese pronunciation is *genyu*. Petroleum is translated into Chinese and Japanese literally as rock oil 石油, pronounced as *shí yóu* in Chinese and *sekiyu* in Japanese.

A plural rather than a collective singular is a much more accurate designation of crude oils because they encompass substances of considerable heterogeneity and vary widely in their appearance, composition, viscosity, flammability, quality and hence in economic usefulness and command commensurately different prices. Moreover, these differences are seen not only among different oilfields but even within sections of a single large oil-bearing rock formation. And as some crude oils are extremely viscous and hardly flow, it is not their liquid state but the shared presence of several series of hydrocarbon compounds that provides the rationale to subsume the extended continuum of oils under a homogenizing singular.

The origins of oils are also sufficiently complex to leave room for two diametrically opposed theories of hydrocarbon formation: the dominant position that sees oils and gases as products of complex, gradual transformations of ancient accumulations of dead organic matter, and the Russian-Ukrainian school of petroleum geology that sees hydrocarbons as abiogenic products, formed under high pressures and temperatures deep in the Earth's mantle from which they rise to be trapped in porous structures near the planet's surface. I will close the chapter by reviewing some essential concepts and processes of petroleum geology such as depositional systems, reservoir rocks and oil migrations and relating these settings and events to the major petroleum provinces and largest oilfields.

Composition of crude oils

Most adults are familiar with the color (or lack of it) and characteristic smell of common refined oil products (gasoline, diesel oil, kerosene, lubricating oils, asphalt) but few have seen crude oils as they come from the ground or as they are carried by tankers and pipelines into refineries. The appearance of crude oils ranges from light, gasoline-like, highly mobile liquids to heavier reddish-brown fluids to highly viscous, tarry black materials. Crude oils are not chemical compounds (hence it is impossible to write down their formulas), they are complex mixtures of scores of hydrocarbons and other minor ingredients. Ultimate elemental analysis of crude oils shows carbon accounting for about 85% (83–87) of their mass and hydrogen for 13% (11–15), with H/C ratios around 1.8, compared to about 0.8 for bituminous coals and four for methane.

The smallest hydrocarbon molecule present in crude oils is gaseous methane, the largest one has more than eighty carbon atoms. Three series of hydrocarbons (whose composition differs by a predictable number of carbon and hydrogen atoms according to a generic formula) dominate the composition of crude oils (see figure 7). Scientific names of these series are alkanes, cycloalkanes, and arenes but in the oil industry they are known as paraffins, cycloparaffins (or napthtenes) and aromatics. Alkanes are the second most abundant homologous series found in crude oils, making up about a quarter of the total mass. Their common name, paraffins (from Latin *parum affinis*, of slight affinity), refers to their inert nature: they do not react with either strong acids or alkaline (or oxygenating) compounds.

They are either straight-chain (normal) or branched-chain molecules; the first group has some sixty members, the other runs theoretically into millions. The two lightest straight-chained alkanes, methane and ethane, are gases at atmospheric pressure. Propane and butane are also gases but are easily compressible to liquids (hence known as liquid petroleum gases, LPG). Chains with five (pentane) to sixteen carbons are liquids, the remainder are solids. Pentane, hexane, and heptane, are normally the most abundant alkanes in crude oils.

Natural gas liquids (NGL) are hydrocarbons that get separated from the gas at special processing facilities: they include ethane, LPG and small amounts of other compounds. Production of NGL is sometimes reported separately from the extraction of crude oil. In 2005 worldwide production of crude oil and condensate was almost 74 Mbpd, and NGL added nearly 8 Mbpd for the total of 81 Mbpd. *Oil & Gas Journal*, one of the industry's leading publications, excludes NGL from its tabulations and hence its 2005 total of global crude oil production was about 10% lower than the statistical series that include NGL (including those of the US government, BP and the UN).

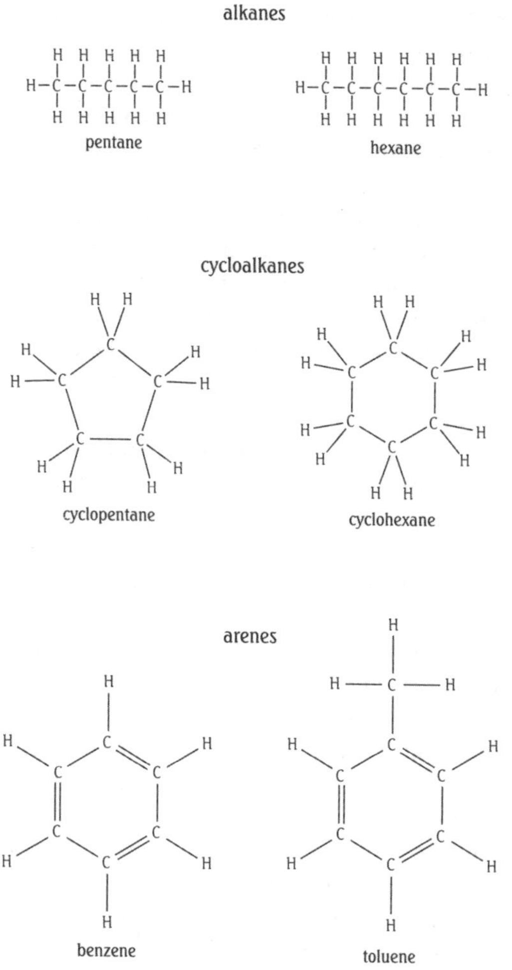

Figure 7 Structures of the most common liquid alkanes, cycloalkanes and arenes.

Cycloalkanes (naphtenes in the oil industry) are the most abundant compounds in crude oil (typically half of the weight), and methylcyclopentane and methylcyclohexane are the two most common cycloalkanes. These saturated hydrocarbons have carbon atoms joined in rings of five (cyclopentane) or six (cyclohexane) atoms which tend to fuse into polycyclic molecules in heavier fractions: bicyclic naphthenes are common in kerosene, tetracyclic and pentacyclic compounds are present in lubricating oil. Arenes (aromatics) are unsaturated, highly reactive liquids named after the members with pleasant odors that share at least one benzene ring to which are attached long, straight side chains. Benzene is the first compound of this series and it is present together with its alkyl derivatives (toluene, ethylbenzene and xylenes). Polycyclic aromatics (naphthalenes, anthracene and phenanthrene) are most common in heavy oils and lubricants and they make up less than 20% of crude oil mass.

Alkenes (olefins) are the most common hydrocarbons in organic matter (present as oils in both plant and animal tissues, but only their traces are found in some crude oils because they are easily reduced to alkanes (in the presence of hydrogen) or to thiols (in the presence of hydrogen sulfide) during the oil's formative period. However, they are produced in quantity during crude oil refining and become major feedstocks in synthetic chemistry. Crude oils also contain nonhydrocarbon compounds (sometime subsumed into a category of asphaltics) whose concentrations are highest in the residue that remains after oil refining. Asphaltics make up less than 10% of crude oil by weight and include compounds of sulfur (usually in sulfides and thiols) and nitrogen (mostly in pyroles, indols and pyridines).

No other hydrocarbons in oil are as structurally remarkable as diamondoids, chair-like arrangement of their carbon atoms produces diamond-like molecules that combine high volatility (as high as that of kerosene) with a relatively very high melting point (higher than that of tin). This extraordinary thermal stability means that their concentrations increase with increasing temperature and that their presence can be used to narrow down the maximum temperatures compatible with the generation of oil hydrocarbons in source rocks and to estimate the degree of oil destruction by natural cracking processes.

Sulfur (ultimately derived from sulfur bonds in proteins of ancient organic matter) is the most common undesirable contaminant of crude oils because its combustion generates sulfur dioxide, a leading precursor of acid rain. 'Sour' oils have more than 2% of sulfur (which means that in residual oils and in asphalt the levels are commonly above 5%), while 'sweet' crude oils have less than 0.5%, with some of them (from Nigeria, Australia and Indonesia) having less than 0.05% S. In addition to dominant hydrocarbon homologues and nonhydrocarbon compounds some crude oils also have relatively high (but in absolute terms only a tiny fraction of 1%) traces of aluminum and heavy metals, including chromium, copper, lead, nickel and vanadium.

VOLUME AND DENSITY: BARRELS AND DEGREES OF API

Differences in oil composition result in specific densities that range mostly between 0.8 and 0.9 grams per milliliter (g/mL, or 800–900 kg/m^3) but whose extremes are about 0.74 and 1.04 g/mL, or as light as a gasoline and slightly heavier than water. This means that one barrel, the standard non-metric volume measure commonly used in the oil industry, has no single mass equivalent. This nineteenth-century container with the volume of 42 US gallons (or roughly 159 litres) was adopted by the US Bureau of the Census in 1872 and it has since been used worldwide for both production statistics and in evaluating oil resources; its common abbreviation is either bbl (for blue barrel) or b (I use the latter in this book).

VOLUME AND DENSITY: BARRELS AND DEGREES OF API (*cont.*)

With heavy crude oils just over six barrels weigh a metric ton (t), with light oils up to 8.5 barrels are needed; most oils fall between 7–7.5 b/t, and the value of 7.33 b/t is the most commonly used average. Because international oil production and reserves continue to be reported in barrels I will use scientific prefixes for their multiples (M for millions, G for billions and T for trillions). Production in barrels per day will be abbreviated as bpd.

Barrel is not the only non-metric unit used by the oil industry: it designates crude oil densities in terms of degrees of the American Petroleum Institute gravity based on an arbitrary assignment of 10 °API to water; conversion from specific density thus follows the general formula °API = (141.5/specific density)-131.5. Consequently, a very heavy crude oil with specific density 0.95 (close to that of water) has °API 17.5, while a light oil with specific density of 0.82 has °API 41. Crude oils with densities above °API 31.1 are classified as light, heavy oils have °API below 22.3. All liquid crude oils are lighter than water and are also immiscible with it and float on its surface: only a strong agitation will produce oil-water emulsion.

Crude oils that dominate the global trade are mostly of medium density or are only moderately light. Most Saudi crude oils rate between °API 28–33, oil from Kuwait's largest oilfield has °API just over 23, the southern Iraqi oil from Basra rates about °API 25. Crude oil from Alaska's North Slope has °API 29 but the North Sea Brent oil has about °API 38. Some Libyan, Algerian and Nigerian oils are very light, with °API 37–44, and the lightest internationally traded crude oil, with °API 60, comes from Australia's Northwestern Shelf. Price is the most obvious marker of crude oil densities: generally, the lighter the oil (the higher the °API), the higher its price.

Straight distillation of lighter oils will produce larger shares of lighter fractions: naphtha can be above 20% for Nigerian light oil and kerosene almost another 20%, with the residue accounting for just a third of total weight; in contrast, distillation of a heavy

Kuwaiti oil will yield less than 25% of naphtha and kerosene and leave nearly two-thirds as a residue. Light oils are naturally preferred by markets that are dominated by gasoline and kerosene demand because their refining needs less catalytic cracking (see chapter 4) to produce the needed mix of products: that is why the US, with its enormous demand for gasoline and jet fuels, is the world's largest importer of light African crude oils.

Oils with high paraffin content tend to have higher shares of waxes and hence elevated pour points. While light crude oils can flow at temperatures as low as -50°C (and commonly at less than -20°C), some high-paraffin crudes will gel even at 40°C and even those with pour points above freezing point may have to be heated before they can be transported in pipelines in cold climates or special additives must be used to lower their viscosity. Daqing oil, from China's largest field, is an example of very waxy crude: it contains about 26% of wax by weight and its gelling point is 32°C.

Because the liquid hydrocarbons forming crude oils have very similar specific heat content (or energy density, that is energy released by the combustion of a unit mass of a substance), the total energy content of different crude oils remains fairly uniform, ranging between 42–44 megajoules per kilogram (MJ/kg), and international energy statistics usually use 42 MJ/kg (or 42 GJ/t) as the mean value when converting fossil fuels to a common energy denominator. This means that energy density of crude oils is about 50% higher than that of the best anthracite coals (29–30 MJ/kg), about twice as high as that of common steam coals (20–24 MJ/kg) that are used for electricity generation, roughly 2.5 times as high as that of air-dry wood (between 16–18 MJ/kg) and four times higher than that of the poorest lignites (brown coals). Low density of gases means that a cubic meter of natural gas will contain about as much energy as a liter (1/1000 of m^3) of crude oil.

Oil's high energy density is perhaps the fuel's most important advantage when compared to coal but there are other notable reasons why liquid fuels have been preferred to solids and why the post-WWII global energy transition from coal to oil has proceeded so rapidly. The already noted higher hydrogen/ carbon ratio of crude oil means that combustion of refined products generates 20–25% less carbon dioxide, the most important green-house gas, per unit of energy than does coal. Although the sulfur content of some crude oils is high, refined products contain much less sulfur than coal and their combustion yields much less sulfur dioxide, the gas most responsible for acidifying deposition (acid rain). And, unlike the burning of coal, combustion of liquid fuels produces only trace amounts of particulate matter.

Other obvious advantages are the ease of long–distance transport: unlike coal, crude oil and refined products can be transported inexpensively, conveniently and very safely by pipelines; and worldwide, very cheaply but with higher risks, by tankers. Unlike coal, liquid fuels are also conveniently stored in large above ground tanks, underground reservoirs or natural caverns filled by pumping. And refined products have a wide range of uses: they can heat homes and industries, generate electricity, power all modes of land, water and air transportation; some oil fractions also have important non-fuel uses as chemical feedstocks and as lubricants and paving materials. Finally, crude oil reaches the surface either because of naturally high reservoir pressure or because of a mechanized artificial lift (mostly by pumping) and its production does not require any dangerous underground work; similarly, refining and distribution processes are highly automated, limiting risky occupational exposures.

Origins of oil

Fossil fuels are organic mineraloids formed by accumulation, burial and transformation of ancient dead biomass, the remnants of terrestrial and aquatic plants and heterotrophic organisms. They are found in the Earth's crust in all three forms of matter, as solids (coals, peats), liquids (crude oils) and natural gases. As already explained, plurals are needed to convey the considerable heterogeneity of their chemical composition and physical properties. All coals were formed through accumulation and transformation of plant mass (phytomass), the product of enzymatically mediated conversion of solar (radiant or electro-magnetic) energy into chemical energy of new plant tissues. These conversions took place in environments akin to today's peat swamp forests of South-East Asia. Often, exquisitely preserved imprints of leaves and fossilized twigs, branches and trunks offer abundant testimonies of this origin.

Photosynthetic conversion is ancient: organic carbon in Archaean sediments puts the first prokaryotic photosynthesizers 3.8 billion years ago, but massive deposits of coal date only from the time when high rates of photosynthesis by large terrestrial plants left behind enormous deposits of dead organic matter. By far the largest coal resources are of Palaeozoic origin (mostly from the Carboniferous period), and most of the rest from the middle and upper Mesozoic era (Jurassic and Cretaceous period) and from the oldest Cenozoic era (from the Paleocene period). Only the poor-quality lignites and peat are the products of the Quaternary period whose oldest sediments were laid down less than 1.8 millions years ago (see figure 8).

Oil's origins are not as easy to trace as those of immobile coal imprinted with visible plant signatures. Oil's mobility means that it is usually found in places where it was not formed and the susceptibility of hydrocarbons to alteration by chemical and physical means led to speculations that it originated from the transformation of coal or by polymerization of gases from basal rocks. There is no doubt that liquid and gaseous hydrocarbons can be formed directly from their constituent atoms by inorganic chemical reactions, specifically by polymerization of methane

Era	Period	Beginning (million years before present)	Notable life milestones
Cenozoic			
Quaternary	Holocene		Civilization
	Pleistocene	1.8	*Homo sapiens*
Tertiary	Pliocene	5.3	*Australopithecus*
	Miocene	23.8	*Ramapithecus*
	Oligocene	33.7	First elephants
	Eocene	54.8	First horses
	Paleocene	65	First primates
Mesozoic	Cretaceous	144	Flowering plants
	Jurassic	206	First birds
	Triassic	248	First mammals
Paleozoic	Permian	290	Reptiles
	Carboniferous	354	Winged insects
	Devonian	417	First sharks
	Silurian	443	First bony fishes
	Ordovician	490	First vertebrates
	Cambrian	543	Trilobites
Proterozoic		2,500	Oxygen rises
Archean		3,800	Bacteria, archaea

All divisions according to the Geological Society of America.

Figure 8 Geological timescale.

precursors but the best isotopic evidence suggests these abiogenic processes do not produce globally significant volumes of crude oils.

Modern consensus among petroleum geologists and geochemists is that oils of inorganic origin are commercially unimportant and that crude oils are derived from dead biomass, from organic compounds formed mostly by monocellular phytoplankton (dominated by cyanobacteria and diatoms) and zooplankton (above all by formaminifera) as well by higher aquatic plants (algae), invertebrates and fish. In addition, terrestrial organic matter, carried by rivers into the ocean, has also been an important contributor of sedimented biomass and many oil formations had their origin in rich lake (lacustrine) environments. Only a small fraction of oil was formed directly by accumulation of biogenic hydrocarbons and their subsequent transformations.

The same hydrocarbons that make up crude oil – alkanes, cycloalkanes and arenes – are present in plants, albeit only in trace quantities and in a very limited variety. Remarkably, plant alkanes have only odd numbers of carbon (15–21 for oceanic species, 25–37 for land plants) in their chains. This oddity is retained in immature source rocks but in crude oils, after the plant hydrocarbon chains were randomly broken up, the odd and even carbon molecules are equal. Terpenes – polymers of isoprene – are another important group of plant hydrocarbons that are commonly encountered as resins (especially in conifers), essentials oils (limonene responsible for citrus scent) and other important compounds, including retinol (vitamin A), and lycopene in tomatoes and carotenes. Some compounds derived from terpenes are considered important biomarkers in crude oil.

Oil appears to be derived mostly from non-hydrocarbon organic molecules that underwent microbial metabolism (bacteriogenesis) and, above all, prolonged thermal decomposition (thermogenesis) after burial in sediments. A recent discovery attests to the ancient origins of this process: abundant nodules of bitumen (dark, inflammable organic matter) and residues of asphaltic pyrobitumen were identified in the black shales of Australia's Pilbara craton, one of the world's least disturbed granite-greenstone rocks that contain some of the oldest known shales. Their presence indicates that crude oil was generated from organic matter in marine sediments as early as 3.2 billion years ago.

Most of the non-hydrocarbon organic compounds belong to one of the three large categories, carbohydrates (with cellulose, a polymer of the simplest sugar, glucose, being the dominant compound in plants), proteins (forming animal and human muscles) and lipids (fats) composed of fatty acids and glycerol. Organisms also contain such metabolic pigments as chlorophyll (responsible for the green color of bacteria, algae and plants) and hemin (in animals); their porphyrin rings (iron centers) are retained in crude oil in nickel and vanadium porphyrin complexes that were formed by reactions with haemoglobin and chlorophyll, and they are considered important markers of oil's biogenic origins. The presence of some identical hydrocarbons in plants and crude oils, structural similarities between plant and animal lipids and oil hydrocarbons and the occurrence of biomarkers confirm oil's organic origins. Many oils also contain fossil spores and pollen.

Most of the world's oil comes not just from sedimentary rocks that were permeated by organic matter but from geological eras known to have exceptionally high photosynthetic productivity, and measurable quantities of oil-like liquid hydrocarbons have been found in a variety of recent marine sediments indicating the continuity of biogenic oil formation. Another notable property arises from the preferential carbon isotope fractionation during photosynthesis: in oil the ratio of two stable isotopes, ^{13}C and the dominant ^{12}C resembles that of plants (photosynthesis preferentially selects the lighter isotope) and not that of carbonate rocks. And the common presence of nitrogen compounds in crude oils is best explained by their organic pedigree: the element is a critical constituent of amino acids that make up proteins.

Organic matter is transformed into oil by a long, sequential process that starts with accumulation of biomass in sedimentary (marine or lacustrine) environments. Initial microbial aerobic degradation returns a significant part of the sediment carbon to the atmosphere as carbon dioxide. Subsequent anaerobic fermentation by methanogenic and sulfate-reducing bacteria releases methane and hydrogen sulfide. Eventual burial of organic matter in anoxic muds leads to the formation of longer-chained compounds and to the generation of kerogens, complex insoluble mixtures of large organic molecules. The kerogen formed mostly from lipids of both marine and terrestrial origins, with H/C ratio <1.25, produces most of the commercially exploited mixtures of crude oil and natural gas.

Kerogen in source rocks (usually shales or limestones) may be as much as 10% of organic matter by weight but contents of 1–2% are typical. The latter suffices to label the rock as a potential candidate for oil generation. With progressive burial of kerogens comes a rise in temperature (the Earth's normal temperature gradient is 25–30°C/km but in many tectonically active regions the rate is much higher) and pressure, and the accumulated organic matter is eventually subjected to thermal degradation (cracking). This process, akin to the production of lighter fuels from heavier fractions in refineries (see chapter 4), breaks up longer-chained molecules and produces lighter compounds. Kerogens change to solid (or almost solid) black or brown macromolecular bitumen whose unmistakable odor betrays its main constituents, heavy hydrocarbons including asphalt and waxes, and the cleavage of bitumen bonds yields complex mixtures of light and heavy hydrocarbon molecules.

Geochemists divide the formation of hydrocarbons from a source rock into three main temperature-dependent stages. Diagenesis (transformation of sediments into sedimentary rocks) is limited to physical and chemical changes that begin at relatively low temperatures of 50–60°C and at depths below 1 km. Catagenesis is the principal process of thermal alteration (cracking) and it is at its most effective within the so called oil window between 65°C and 150°C, with the ratio of gas/oil formation increasing as the temperature rises with most of oil's complex constituents produced at temperatures between 80°C and 120°C. Metamorphic processes are thermal alterations in environments hotter than 200°C. The oil window can also be defined in terms of depth: where the thermal gradient is high (> 5°C) the minimum overburden can be less than 1 km, in formations with low thermal gradient the oil window may extend to below 8 km, with optimum oil-producing conditions between about 2.2 and 4.5 km.

Source rocks exposed only to lower temperatures are considered to be immature, those processed extensively at temperatures above 200°C are overmature, crude oil constituents become unstable and dry gas (that is basically pure methane) is the principal product. The rate of oil generation is also affected by the pressure and the presence of heat-tolerant or outright thermophilic bacteria. Hydrogen and oxygen derived from water and surrounding minerals also participate in these transformations, as do catalytically active transition metals. Some hydrocarbon reservoirs yield only negligible volumes of gases while at the other extreme (where the processing temperatures approached the upper range of the window) there is only natural gas and during the decades preceding its common commercial use drillers were disappointed to find it and vented or flared nearly all of it.

Most of the oil formed during the past half a billion years was degraded by thermophilic bacteria resident in oil reservoirs and active in temperatures up to about 80°C. These microbes, metabolizing very slowly and acting on geological timescales of millions of years, are able to destroy many of oil's components and produce much denser heavy oils. These biodegraded oils, rather than the Middle Eastern deposits of hydrocarbon liquids, dominate the world's resources and their largest concentrations are in shallow reservoirs situated on the eastern flank of the American Cordillera. These foreland basins – Western Canada basin in Alberta and Saskatchewan with its heavy oils and tars, and the Eastern Venezuelan basin (the Orinoco tar belt) – are the world's largest petroleum accumulations, each containing in the order of 1 Tb of oil (see chapter 5 regarding their exploitation).

Oil generation is clearly a multifactorial and highly protracted process. While the best environment for the formation of crude oils was in the areas that combined generally high photosynthetic productivity with high rates of undisturbed accumulation (deposition) even such ideal conditions would only rarely produce a single massive layer of source rocks because the periods of enhanced photosynthesis (supported by an elevated influx of nutrients) alternated with times of slower growth. Subsequent burial may have been too slow, leading to large aerobic oxidation of the accumulated biomass, and thermal processing could be inadequate or excessive.

Given the abundance of dead organic matter that entered sediments during the past half billion years and the adequate time that has been available for transforming these remains to liquid fuels it is clear that the process of oil formation is relatively inefficient. The generation of substantial oil deposits required enormous inputs of primordial organic matter, with no known commercially exploitable oil formations being younger than the time elapsed from the peak of the latest glaciation, and with the oldest ones dating back to the Palaeozoic era. Approximate comparisons with the generation of coal indicate the extraordinary demand of this process: roughly 1,000 times more ancient biomass was needed to transfer a unit of carbon from organic matter to crude oil than was required to preserve it in coal.

Up to this point I have reviewed our understanding of oil's origins based on the prevailing consensus of Western geologists and geochemists – but I should note that an alternative theory of oil's origins has been available since the early 1950s, an intriguing Russian-Ukrainian hypothesis about the abyssal abiogenic origin of hydrocarbons. This is not yet another example of a

PHOTOSYNTHETIC (CARBON) COST OF COAL AND OIL

Coal formation has high carbon preservation rates. Close to 15% of the element is transferred from plants to peat and 75–95% of that carbon ends up as coal. Underground coal mining usually removes about 50% of coal in place and surface mining takes out as much as 90%. The overall carbon recovery factor (the share of the element's original presence in phytomass that ends up in marketable fuel) is thus as high as 20% for lignites and as low as 2% for the best anthracites, with rates around 10% being typical for the most commonly mined bituminous coals. Obversely, this means that 5–50 units of carbon locked in ancient plant mass were needed to produce one unit of carbon in coal.

In comparison to coal formation, preservation factors of carbon were lower during the formation of marine and lacustrine sediments (rarely over 10% , often less than 1%), and much lower during the subsequent heating and pressurization of organic sediments. Published data also indicate a much wider range of preservation factors and crude oil also has much lower extraction factors than coal: commonly just 10–20% of all carbon originally present in oil formations ends up on the market. This means that the mean overall recovery factor for crude oil carbon is less than 0.01%. On the average some 10,000 units of carbon (or as few as about 100 and as many as 300,000 or more) in the initially sequestered biomass were needed to produce a unit of carbon in marketed crude oil. Refining further lowers this recovery factor and a memorable encapsulation of these calculations is that every liter of gasoline (about 740 g containing about 640 g of carbon) represents some 25 t of originally sequestered marine biomass.

deranged Stalinist science (like Lysenkoist genetics): the theory is based on theoretical considerations as well as on extensive field observations and it has been criticized and discussed for decades in more than four thousand papers, book chapters and books. Most importantly, the theory has guided extensive exploratory drilling that has resulted in the discovery of oil and its production from crystalline basement rocks in scores of hydrocarbon fields in the Caspian Sea region, western Siberia and the Dnieper-Donets Basin.

ABIOGENIC THEORY

Russian and Ukrainian scientists have argued that the standard account, calling for the formation of highly reduced high energy density hydrocarbons from highly oxidized low energy density organic molecules, violates the second law of thermodynamics and that the formation of such highly reduced molecules requires high pressures that are encountered only in the Earth's mantle. In 2002 Jason F. Kenney of the Gas Resources Corporation in Houston – a leading American advocate of this theory who also works at the Russian Academy of Sciences – and his Russian colleagues published the result of experiments that produced an entire suite of petroleum fluids in a special apparatus that mimicked the conditions 100 km below the Earth's surface by operating under high pressure (fifty MPa) and temperature (up to 1500°C). Although the paper appeared in the *Proceedings of the National Academy of Sciences* its publication did not lead to any widespread adoption of the theory.

Proponents of abiogenic theory point out not only many weaknesses in the dominant explanation but they also refer to what they see as 'pure and simple' cases of intellectual fraud. Fossil spores and pollen found in oil can be explained by leaching from buried organic matter; specific carbon isotope ratios can be explained by the age of hydrocarbon deposits and their migration paths; porphyrins, isoprenoids and other organic molecules do not have to come from ancient biomass as they have been found in dozens of meteorites. Thomas Gold, a leading US astronomer and geoscientist and the theory's best known Western advocate, pointed out the existence of abiogenic hydrocarbons on other planetary bodies and argued that on Earth, hydrocarbons can be made from hydrogen and carbon under the high temperatures and

ABIOGENIC THEORY (*cont.*)

pressures of the outer mantle. This would also explain why these compounds almost always contain elevated levels of inert helium.

Advocates of abiogenic theory also argue that giant oilfields (containing more than 500 Mb of recoverable oil) are better explained by oil's inorganic origins rather than by postulating enormous accumulations of organic matter.

This theory has equally passionate advocates and detractors. However, skeptics should recall that most geologists resisted for several generations an idea that suddenly became (during the 1960s) a key paradigm of their science: the theory of plate tectonics that had been championed by Alfred Wegener, a German meteorologist, since the 1920s. And they should also be reminded that another one of Gold's controversial ideas – the existence of bacteria deep underground (what he called deep hot biosphere) that was ridiculed by the geological and biological establishment when first published – has now been incontrovertibly confirmed by experimental drilling.

Geology of hydrocarbon deposits

Commercial viability of oil deposits is determined by the great trinity of hydrocarbon geology, the right combination of a rich source rock, a permeable and porous reservoir rock and a suitable tight trap to hold the liquid in place. The genesis of a source rock and sediment with a relatively high content of organic matter, is controlled by interactions of three rates, those of production, destruction and dilution. All of them are, in turn, governed (often in a non-linear fashion) by a multitude of external factors, each one can fluctuate across at least an order of magnitude, and only their appropriate combination will result in high accumulation rates. Additional factors that have a major influence on the rate of organic matter accumulation are the sulfurization of organic molecules and their adsorption onto (or within) clay particles: both processes make the molecules less vulnerable to oxidation and increase the probability of their preservation.

Primary (photosynthetic) productivity in marine environments depends critically on the availability of nutrients (in all aquatic environments particularly on the fluxes of nitrogen, phosphorus and iron) in the photic zone (part of the water column penetrated by sunlight) and on the concentrations of atmospheric CO_2. In turn, nutrient concentrations are determined by the intensity and extent of oceanic upwelling (transfer of deeper, nutrient-rich waters to the surface) and on nutrient transport by rivers while the secular fluctuations of CO_2 (driven by orbital, geotectonic and climatic factors) often result in an obvious cyclicity of deposition.

High productivity was more likely to overwhelm the destruction rate and result in net deposition of dead biomass but it alone could not guarantee substantial deposition as it could be largely negated by excessive dilution. Destruction of deposited organic matter (largely through its degradation by microorganisms and return of carbon to the atmosphere as CO_2) is primarily the function of oxygen concentrations: in oxic settings its rates are one or even two magnitudes faster than in dysoxic or anoxic environments. Consequently, the presence of anoxic bottom water has often been considered as the main controlling factor for organic matter preservation. The decay function is nonlinear and only the settings with less than one milliliter of oxygen per liter had a chance to accumulate significant amounts of dead biomass.

Dilution, that is organic carbon-free sedimentation, can be extremely variable, spanning four orders of magnitude and amounting to as much as 20 kg/m^2. Sedimentation that can create optimal conditions for the preservation and subsequent processing of accumulated biomass is a matter of a delicate balance between desirable rates of burying the organic matter (and hence isolating it from oxygen) and lowering the sediment's organic content below the levels capable of producing oil rich source rocks. In marine ecosystems high rates of dilution can also result from high photosynthetic productivity that contributes a relatively large mass of hydrogen-poor tests, shells and bones. For example, most of the mass of coccolithophorids (single-celled planktonic protists) is their intricately-built calcium carbonate armor (see figure 9).

Accumulations of organic matter, and hence the generation of source rocks, were not spread evenly through geological eras but were clearly concentrated in a limited number of intervals whose duration and recurrence were determined primarily by global geotectonic cycles and secondarily by planetary climate changes driven by orbital oscillations. The total mass of organic matter stored in the Earth's crust is on the order of 10^{16} tons, with 10^{14} t (100 Tt) in organic–rich rocks, principally shales containing at least 3% of organic matter (the range is from fractions of a per cent to as much as 40% for oil source rocks and nearly 100% in some types of coal).

An approximate secular division of this global accumulation indicates that different geological eras contributed the following shares of the world's kerogens:

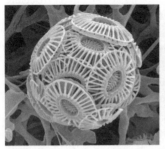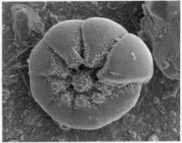

Figure 9 The intricate carbonate armor of a coccolithophorid (*Emiliania huxleyi*) and a foraminiferan protist (*Ammonia parkinsoniana*).

- Nearly 30% from the mid-Cretaceous period (about 100 million years ago).
- 25% from the late Jurassic period (around 150 million years ago).
- Less than 10% each from the late Devonian (350 million years ago), Silurian (408–438 million years ago) and early Cambrian (about 550 million years ago) periods.

The mid and late Mesozoic eras are thus the source of more than half of all kerogen and hence, not surprisingly, of a similar share of oil originally in place in the uppermost sliver of the Earth's crust. When burning refined oil products we are thus primarily converting a planetary patrimony that remained undisturbed for more than 100 million years.

The next step in the genesis of exploitable oil resources is the release of hydrocarbons from the kerogen beds where they were formed and the movement of crude oils (migration) from fairly (or highly) impermeable source rocks to relatively highly permeable reservoir rocks, and eventually to the Earth's surface and hence to oil's inevitable bacterially-mediated decomposition. We will never know how much oil had made it that far during the elapsed geological eras and was rather rapidly decomposed: we deal only with that still imperfectly known fraction that was confined in reservoir rocks by a variety of traps and that we discover by geophysical exploration and drilling (see chapter 3).

During the primary migration, oil is expelled from its source rock and although water is always present this transport through pores and capillaries does not always take the form of a solution or emulsion (oil being fairly immiscible) but it is one of an independent movement driven by the pressure of overburden rocks and made easier by the presence of faults and fractures. Oil expelled from its source rocks represents only a tiny fraction of migrating liquids (on the order of $10^{-2}\%$) and it is also highly dispersed, as organic-rich source rocks of a single formation may cover hundreds of square kilometers. Secondary migration, proceeding through much more permeable media of porous rocks and driven largely by oil's buoyancy, concentrates it by carrying it to one of the many possible traps where it accumulates. Tertiary migration (leaks, seepages) leads oil from traps to the surface. When migrating hydrocarbons lose their volatile components they become heavy and non-liquid and the crust contains large volumes of these semi-solid or solid materials.

Virtually all commercially viable oil reservoirs are products of migration: *in situ* origin of oil in trapped reservoir rocks is highly unlikely as it would require the source rocks to be situated within traps. The word reservoir invokes images of large liquid pools but underground pools of oil are extremely rare. Instead, a reservoir is any subsurface body of rock whose porosity and permeability are sufficient to store and to transmit fluids so they are eventually able to flow into a borehole. Reservoir shapes are determined by the subsurface structures or discontinuities that envelope them or delimit them and they can range from relatively shallow irregularly shaped near-horizontal lenses to steep wedge-like enclosures.

Porosity is the share of void space in the reservoir rock that can be filled by hydrocarbons and, of course, also by water and non-hydrocarbon gases. High porosity may be created during the rock's deposition (primary porosity) or it can arise through a later alteration of the formation (secondary porosity due to recrystallization or fracturing). However, isolated pores would preclude oil extraction and hence it is the effective porosity, the volume of interconnected pores in a rock that determines eventual productivity. Sedimentary rocks are generally much more porous than even the most fractured igneous or metamorphic formations and sandstones and carbonates (limestones and dolostones) are by far the most common reservoir rocks. Their porosity ranges from less than 10% to about 70% (in some limestones) of the rock's total volume, with typical shares between 20–30%.

Permeability quantifies a rock's capacity to transmit fluids. Permeable rocks have a multitude of relatively large and abundantly connected pores, impermeable formations (shales being a good example) have much smaller and poorly connected pores. As with the porosity, effective permeability, the capacity to transmit a fluid when other fluids are present, is a more telling indicator. Permeability, measured in darcy units (D), can range over four orders of magnitude, from 0.1 mD to more than 10 D. Such impermeable rocks as salt, shales and anhydrite (calcium sulfate, a soft rock created by the evaporation of seawater) are able to keep reservoir rocks sealed through geological eras because their permeability is merely 10^{-6} to 10^{-8} D. Reservoir rocks with good porosity and permeability are classed in two broad categories, those of clastic and carbonate systems.

CLASTIC AND CARBONATE SEDIMENTS

Clastic sediments are formed from fragments of various rocks that were transported and redeposited to create new formations: sandstones, siltstones and shales are the most common examples. Clastic deposition leads eventually to sandstone reservoirs and many distinct processes result in such accretions. Alluvial fans accumulate different sizes of eroded matter as mountain streams debauch onto open, flatter ground. This intermittent deposition has only rarely produced giant reservoirs: Venezuela's Quiriquire is perhaps the most notable example. Rivers deposit substantial volumes of sand and gravel particularly when they flow as braided or meandering streams. Alaska's Prudhoe Bay originated as a Triassic sandstone deposit in a braided flow.

Sedimentation in lakes has produced only a limited number of major oil reservoirs, most notably in China. In contrast, sedimentary rocks that originated as submarine fans harbor such rich oil reservoirs as the Forties field in the North Sea. But no other clastic depositional systems have contributed as many reservoir rocks as

CLASTIC AND CARBONATE SEDIMENTS (*cont.*)

river deltas, ranging from elongated and lobate formations to wave-dominated forms: at least two-fifths of global oil production has come from deltaic sediments. Notably, the Tertiary deposits along the US Gulf coast, a number of Venezuelan coastal fields, the Niger delta and the south Caspian Sea. Shallow marine flats are also ideal depositional settings, often producing source rocks in association with reservoir rocks: fields in the central part of the North Sea have this origin.

Many of the world's largest reservoirs are in carbonate rocks. These are formed either inorganically, through a chemical reaction (precipitation) of seawater calcium and carbonate ions in shallow seas, or by the process of biomineralization whereby marine organisms produce large carbonate structures (reef-building corals) or a constant rain of tiny shells and test: algal coccolithophorids and foraminiferal protists are the most common biomineralizers (see figure 9). Calcite and aragonite, two chemically identical compounds (calcium carbonate) with different crystal structures, dominate limestone composition. Partial replacement of calcium by magnesium (from evaporating seawater or during a deep burial) creates dolomite, the principal constituent of dolostones, whose higher porosity makes for excellent reservoir rocks. Carbonates can also be fragmented and redeposited as clastic sediments.

Most of these sediments originated in shallow sea waters (shelves) and their simplest subdivision is into ramps (with gently sloping sides) and platforms (flat, with sharply sloping sides). The world's largest oil reservoirs in the Persian Gulf produce from Jurassic or Cretaceous shelf limestones. The Permian grainstones of West Texas and south-eastern New Mexico form the most productive onshore oil province in the continental US, while Alberta's giant oilfields are outstanding examples of production from Devonian reefs. Dolomitic reservoirs are also widely distributed, with the most productive ones (from the upper Jurassic) in the Arabian platform. Deep water carbonates are much less common (Mexico's Poza Rica and the North Sea's Ekofisk are outstanding examples), as are karst reservoirs (notably in buried hills in China).

Oil in reservoirs is contained by various traps, upwardly rising curves or angled containments, that can originate through a variety of structural and stratigraphic processes and that are sealed by highly impermeable rocks, most often by shales or evaporites (see figure 10). Structural traps are formed by deformations of the Earth's crust. Anticlines, smooth arch-shaped (convex) folds, make such outstanding hydrocarbon traps that they enclose nearly four-fifths of the world's largest oil reservoirs. Some anticlinal traps have reservoir rocks situated right in the middle (the core) of the convex shape where they are capped by impermeable strata. Anticlinal structures can be both large and almost perfectly symmetrical (seen as ovals on topographic maps) or can be closed by faults (relative displacements of rock strata that prevent further oil migration) including normal, reverse and strike-slip arrangements.

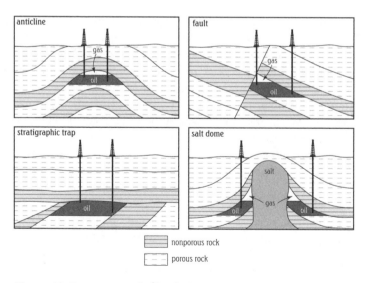

Figure 10 Four common kinds of oil traps.

The most extensive structural traps are formed by compressive tectonics along convergent plate boundaries. Such contractional folds, created by the Miocene collision of Arabia with Eurasia, produced an entire system of two spectacular asymmetric whaleback anticlines (Lurestan and Fars) in the Zagros Fold Belt of Iran. In between is the Dezful Embayment – a depression some 600 km long running in a NW-SE direction and up to 200 km wide with a total area of some 50,000 km^2 – that harbors forty-five oilfields, including such supergiant reservoirs (containing more than 5 Gb of recoverable oil) as Agha Jari, Ahwaz, Bibi Hakimeh, Gachsaran and Marun. Source rocks of these fields are an early Tertiary (Paleocene and Eocene) Pabdeh formation and a mid-Cretaceous Kazhdumi deposit, and the two main reservoir rocks are the Sarvak formation (overlaying Kazhdumi) and the Miocene Asmari rocks capped by Gachsaran evaporates. Another large-scale anticlinal trap contains oil in eastern Venezuela.

Other remarkable structural traps are created, albeit on a smaller scale than tectonic anticlines, by diapirs, vertical intrusions of lighter formations through denser rocks. Because salt (halite) has a lower density than the surrounding sedimentary rocks (2.2 vs. at least 2.5 g/cm^3) it is buoyant and as it rises through sedimentary formations it can be plastically deformed, creating domes, sheets or pillars. Anticlinal structures generated by rising salt domes create excellent traps on their own and they are also often associated with evaporite rocks (gypsum, anhydrite) that provide perfect caps and seals. Reservoir rocks are frequently found draping over a rising salt, with steep side dips. Diapiric anticlines can be also formed by rising hot magma (but the heat generated by their rise would be likely to destroy the hydrocarbons present in the reservoir rock), shales and movements of mud. The world's second largest oilfield, Kuwaiti al-Burqān, is a Cretaceous sandstone trapped above a massive (roughly 750 km^2) salt swell.

Stratigraphic traps are generally on smaller scales, resulting from gradual accretions of impermeable rocks that enclose oil-bearing formations (depositional traps) and from sudden unconformities (created by erosion or by karst phenomena). They also arise from mineral precipitation, dissolution, intrusion of tar mats or permafrost. Primary stratigraphic traps include such elongated sandstone bodies as point bars, deltaic channels and barriers as well as carbonate slopes and coral reefs. Secondary stratigraphic traps come as various unconformities, clay-filled channels of diagenetic dolomites or calcites. Stratigraphic traps are often present as multiple, complex, staggered phenomena, and they are also often combined with structural traps. Major oilfields with stratigraphic traps include Alaska's Prudhoe Bay, East Texas, Bolívar Coastal and Venezuela's supergiant along the east coast of Lake Maracaibo that is bounded by an enormous tar seal.

AL-GHAWĀR OILFIELD

Some of the principal concepts of petroleum geology that have been introduced in this chapter are illustrated here in describing the essential features of al-Ghawār, the world's largest supergiant oilfield that was discovered in north-eastern Saudi Arabia about 80 km inland from the western coast of the Persian Gulf. Al-Ghawār's extraordinary size and its high sustained productivity are due to a nearly perfect combination of a large structure sourced from a prolific formation into a highly permeable reservoir capped by an excellent seal. The field is a large (250 km long and about 30 km wide) gentle anticline with two subparallel crests (separated by a saddle) that is draped over a horst, an elevated deformation of the basement rock that arose originally during the Carboniferous period (see figure 11).

Both the source and reservoir rocks belong to the Upper Jurassic Shaqra group. Ghawār's source rock is a highly prolific, organic-rich lime mudstone of the Tuwaiq Mountain Formation (with about 3.5% of total organic carbon), about 150 m thick that was laid down

AL-GHAWĀR OILFIELD (*cont.*)

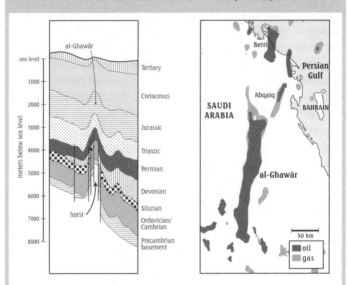

Figure 11 East-west cross-section of strata at al-Ghawār, the world's largest oilfield, and the field's extent.

in intershelf basins between 164–155 million years ago. The overlying Hanifa formation (with about 2.5% of organic carbon) also contributed to the original store of organic matter. Because of the great oil volume in place it is likely that a major lateral migration took place before the oil migrated a short vertical distance to the reservoir rock, late Jurassic Arab-D limestone laid down between 150–145 million years ago that lies 1.8–2.1 km below the surface.

This rock is up to 120 m thick and its quality improves from the bottom mudstone to clean top grainstone. Its porosity exceeds 30% in some parts of the reservoir (mean of 14–18%) and its permeability is also excellent (in parts more than 600 mD). The oil-bearing limestones are capped by a massive (up to 150 m thick) layer of impermeable anhydrite of the late Jurassic Hith formation that is not broken by any major faults.

Most large commercial oilfields produce from relatively young reservoir rocks. Approximate division by geological periods puts almost 45% of all reservoir rocks to the Jurassic and 35% to the Cretaceous period while reservoirs dating to the late Paleozoic periods (Silurian to Permian) are relatively uncommon. A classification by major producing oilfields shows that just over half of their reservoir rocks are Mesozoic, nearly 40% are early Cenozoic and less than 10% are Paleozoic. The youngest known oil-bearing sediments (in the US, in Texas and Louisiana) are less than 20,000 years old, contemporary with the peak of the last Ice Age.

As for the major oil provinces, their dating (going backwards in time) is as follows:

- Mid-late Cretaceous source rocks are found in China's Songliao Basin (the site of Daqing, the country's largest supergiant field), in the Gulf of Mexico, the Persian Gulf, Venezuela and in waters off Congo.
- Upper Jurassic layers are productive in Western Siberia, the Persian Gulf and the North Slope of Alaska.
- Late Jurassic rocks occur in the Gulf of Mexico, the North Slope of Alaska, the North Sea, Western Siberia, the Persian Gulf and Northern Caucasus.
- Triassic, early Permian to late Carboniferous basins include China's Tarim and Junggar and the southern part of the North Sea.
- Early Carboniferous to late Devonian sediments produced such important oil provinces as Russia's Volga-Ural and Timan–Pechora, West Canadian Sedimentary Basin, Oklahoma and Texas.

This distribution, with commercially exploitable resources of oil present on all continents, makes it difficult to make any grand simplifying generalizations. One intriguing observation is that the world's largest oil-bearing basins are concentrated either along the shores of the Mesozoic Tethys Ocean that was wedged between the supercontinents of Laurasia (to the north) and Gondwana, extending from today's Indonesia through the Middle East to North Africa, or along both flanks of the American Cordillera, from Alberta through the Gulf of Mexico to Trinidad, Venezuela and Brazil and, on the western side, from Alaska through California to Ecuador. On the other hand, size distribution of the world's oil resources makes it possible to make a number of fascinating observations.

The size of oil reservoirs shares a highly skewed (geometric) frequency distribution with many of the Earth's discrete physical features: for example there is only one Greenland, and just two islands of the size of New Guinea and Borneo, thousands of small islands and myriads of tiny reefs and islets. Similarly skewed frequency distributions can be plotted for the size of lakes or the length of peninsulas – or for the sizes of oilfields: most of the world's commercially exploited oilfields hold only small volumes of oil (and there is, obviously, a much larger number of even smaller reservoirs that are not worth exploiting) while a small number of giant and supergiant reservoirs contain a disproportionately large share of the oil present in the Earth's crust.

At the beginning of the 21st century there were – depending on how some contiguous or adjacent structures are classified, and also on the uncertain estimates of ultimately recoverable oil – at least 600 or more than 700 giant oilfields in twenty different regions, and nearly forty of these were supergiants. Giant fields contained at least 65% of all crude oil reserves, and the supergiants alone claimed nearly one half, with the largest one (Saudi al-Ghawār) holding nearly 10%, and the five largest supergiants – al-Ghawār, Kuwaiti al-Burqān, Mexico's Cantarell, Venezuela's Bolívar and the Saudi Safānīya-Khafjī – having approximately a quarter of the world's oil reserves. I must stress that all of these shares are not only rounded approximations but that they also change with continuing reappraisals of ultimately recoverable oil in producing fields; these are the consequence of additional drilling and higher recovery rates and commonly result in substantial additions to initially estimated reserve totals.

Spatial distribution of the world's largest oil fields is also highly skewed: the Persian Gulf region contains more than half of all supergiants and nearly 30% of all giants. Western Siberia has about 12% and the Gulf of Mexico nearly 10% of all giants. The regions with approximately 5% of the world's giants include the Anadarko/Permian Basin in Oklahoma, Texas and New Mexico, the Volga-Urals, the Caspian Sea, and South-East Asia (Thailand, Indonesia and Vietnam). Regions with fewer than ten giants include North Alaska, Brazil, the Black Sea, Siberia, north-western Australia and the Bass Strait. Production figures show similar disparities.

By 2005 some 120 giants – or fewer than 3% of the more than 4,000 oilfields that were in production in 2005 – accounted for nearly half of all global oil extraction. Classification based on the basin type confirms the already noted absence of a dominant pattern: about 30% of giants are situated along passive continental margins, another 30% are along continental rifts and nearly 25% are found along continental collisional margins. In the future there may be some pleasant surprises as we discover more giants than is currently anticipated, but the global pattern of oil distribution will remain essentially unchanged, a constancy that will maintain the dominance of the Middle Eastern producers.

3

How oil is found and where it has been discovered

The search for mineral resources is an inherently difficult and commercially risky enterprise. Compared to many deposits of metallic ores that are found in thin and twisting veins deep underground, many oil reservoirs are massive structures that lie fairly close to the surface. Some, signalled by surface pools, seeps or gas vents, were discovered without any of the sophisticated geophysical tools and procedures that are available to modern explorers, but many remarkable innovations were required to find smaller and deeper reservoirs. These advances have ranged from better theoretical understanding of the geology of oil-bearing formations and clever exploratory techniques to complex three- and four-dimensional (3D, 4D) simulations and visualizations of oil reservoir dynamics.

Eventually, exploration wells have to be sunk to verify the presence of significant volumes of oil, but given the cost of drilling (increasingly in remote continental locations that are often very difficult to access, in deeper and stormy offshore waters, and at greater depths, both onshore and in what is now called ultradeep ocean drilling) it has become imperative to minimize the risk of repeatedly ending up with dry wells. But even with the advanced geophysical methods that provide unprecedented knowledge about the formation to be drilled, every new exploratory well (and particularly those in promising but previously undrilled locations) still justifies the oil industry's traditional name for such an undertaking, a wildcat. The main reason for this is that none of the parameters of an explored oil formation, and particularly not its pressure configuration, are known with certainty and drilling crews must be prepared for unexpected kicks (inflows of reservoir fluids, water, oil or gas, into a well bore during its progress) that may lead to violent well blowouts.

After a brief history of oil exploration and the drilling methods used to discover oil, and a more detailed description of current drilling tools and practices, I will turn to historical accounts of oilfield discoveries. Most of the drilling – starting with the world's first wells that were completed explicitly in search of oil during the 1850s, proceeding through the pioneering exploration decades of the late nineteenth century, culminating in the discovery of most of the giant oilfields that are in production today, and continuing in the still inadequately explored regions of the Earth – has been done on land, but many remarkable advances in exploratory offshore drilling created a new (post-WWII) industry without which the world would now be missing nearly a third of its crude oil supply.

Geophysical exploration

Early explorers for oil had little to guide them: obvious surface signs of oil's presence (such as natural seeps or pools, tarry rocks or tar lakes) were uncommon, subtler geochemical indicators were not well understood and hunches and guesses were a costly way to decide where to drill. But eventually oil exploration adopted and adapted techniques of geophysical investigation, above all the studies of the Earth's natural electrical, gravitational and magnetic fields and of the propagation of seismic (elastic) waves through the Earth's crust. Reflection seismology, a key

HISTORY OF SEISMIC EXPLORATION

The seismic search for oil had its origins in Reginald Fessenden's research on detecting icebergs and locating ore bodies (patented in 1917) and in the independent invention of practical, albeit initially crude, seismographs. The first portable device was invented by Ludger Mintrop during WWI in order to give the German army a highly accurate means of locating the positions of Allied artillery. In the US John C. Karcher developed a reflection seismograph at the federal Bureau of Standards after the end of WWI and the first field test of the device (on 4 June 1921) confirmed that seismic techniques can unveil the existence of oil-bearing structures. In 1926 his crew located a promising structure around Seminole in Oklahoma and on 4 December 1928 the first well ever to be drilled by following the results of reflection seismography struck oil. In 1930 Karcher founded the Geophysical Service Company which was to become Texas Instruments (later, a leader in microelectronics).

Reflection seismography became much more sensitive with the use of vacuum tubes and, since the early 1950s, with the adoption of transistors. The decade's other innovations included electronic data recording and processing, Harry Mayne's signal-to-noise enhancing technique, and Conoco's vibroseis method that substituted waves created by vibration or weight dropping for waves generated by dynamite explosions. In the late 1960s Mike Forrest, a Shell geophysicist, discovered that strong seismic reflections ('bright spots') on the crest of hydrocarbon-bearing formations make it possible to use seismic data for the direct detection of oil and gas formations. Digitalization and computerization of seismography also started during the 1960s and advanced during the 1970s; at the same time, oil exploration's enormous demand for data acquisition and processing was among a few key factors that pushed the performance of new hardware and required complex new software. The most remarkable sign of this interplay was the introduction of three-dimensional (3D) seismic surveys. The technique was pioneered by Exxon in the Friendswood oilfield near Houston in 1967 and it became routine by the mid-1970s.

exploratory tool, maps subsurface deposits by clocking the time needed for a pulse sent underground to return to the surface after it has been reflected from the interfaces formed by different types of rock formations.

All seismic surveys use the same basic procedure: they generate sound waves at the surface (using truck-mounted vibration pads or, where trucks cannot be driven, dynamite charges in shallow holes) and an array of sensitive receivers (geophones) to record the sound waves reflected from rock formations. In marine exploration the sound waves are generated from air guns (firing compressed air) that are towed on a line behind a ship and reflections are recorded by hydrophones located further down the line (see figure 12).

Standard three-component seismic surveys determine the type of wave and the direction of its propagation by using three orthogonally oriented geophones; hydrophones are added to

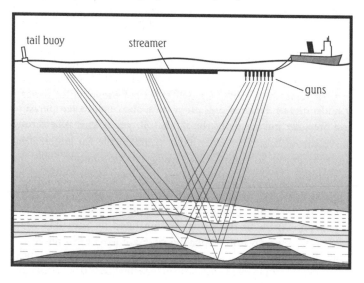

Figure 12 Simplified diagram of a marine seismic survey.

ocean-bottom sensors to measure additional waves for a four-component seismic survey. The massive amounts of data are then processed by high-speed computers. The resulting 3D maps provide unprecedented insights into the structure of subsurface formations and hence about the best ways to exploit them. Increased computing power (driven by Moore's famous law of doubling the capacity of the microprocessor every 18 months) was an essential ingredient of the 3D seismic revolution as the amount of raw data that had to be interpreted for a typical survey increased more than 5,000-fold!

Another computing advance that revolutionized oil exploration and called for an unprecedented amount of data processing capacity was the development of 3D visualization. Arco, Texaco and Norsk Hydro were the first companies to use large immersive visualizations whereby the experts are enveloped by tall projection screens or, even more impressively, enter visualization rooms where they are literally surrounded by data through which they can walk and while virtually immersed in an oil reservoir they can chose the best location and paths for new wells. And this process has been carried yet another step forward with the development of time-lapse 4D seismic surveys.

Repeated monitoring of a reservoir over a period of weeks or months unveils its changing properties, above all its temperature and pressure and the paths the fluids (oil, water, gas) take as they move through it. This knowledge is invaluable for anticipating future reservoir flows and hence siting new production wells, for identifying oil or gas bearing areas that have been bypassed by existing wells and that are worth returning to, and for accelerating and enhancing existing hydrocarbon recovery. Not every 4D survey results in the gains demonstrated in Sumatra's Duri field, where the optimized placing of steamflood wells raised the rate of reservoir recovery from just 8% to nearly 60%, but rewards are always substantial. Crosswell seismic surveys are another new tool that sharpens the understanding of reservoir structure and flow – acoustic sources are deployed in one well bore and the propagated wave recorded in another.

During the early decades of oil exploration the drillers did not even have any reliable means to determine the progress of their operations. A cumbersome and expensive way to get that information was to periodically use a special drill that cut a slim cylindrical core of solid rock that was brought to the surface for examination. This is still done when a periodic examination of actual rock core samples is required: an expensive hollow diamond-covered drill is used to remove cylinders of rock for a preliminary appraisal in the field or more detailed evaluation in a laboratory. A cheaper alternative is sidewall coring, using either a small explosive charge to propel a tiny core barrel sideways from the well or a small robotic core bit to drill short (up to 5 cm), thin rock core samples withdrawn by a wireline.

Recording the kinds of rocks and their attributes based on the samples of rock cuttings (so called mud logs) is an easier option than coring, and this logging, together with the measuring of the rate of penetration, became the first step toward getting a systematic record of the changing properties of rock formations. Eventually these records became automated and modern well logs inform on variables ranging from the speed of rotation and hoisting to the mud flow rate and pressure and temperature at the bottom of the well. The single biggest advance in oil exploration came in 1911 when Conrad Schlumberger, at that time a lecturer at the French École des Mines, came up with the novel idea of using electrical conductivity measurements in prospecting for metallic ore deposits. A year later his first crude map of equipotential curves indicated that the technique could also be used to identify subsurface structures that could act as traps for such mobile resources as oil and gas.

The process of electric well logging pioneered by Schlumberger is one of the mainstays of modern geophysical exploration: it consists of measuring a number of revealing

WELL LOGGING

Société de Prospection Electrique, the precursor of today's Schlumberger Company, was set up in 1926 and it rapidly expanded its operations to the Americas, Asia and the USSR. In 1927 Henri Doll, an experimental physicist, produced the first electrical resistivity well log, a record of successive resistivity readings that are used to create a resistivity curve. In 1930 the company introduced a continuous hand recorder and a year later Conrad, together with his brother Marcel Schlumberger and E.G. Leonardon, recognized the phenomenon of spontaneous potential that is generated naturally between the borehole fluid electrode and the formation water in permeable beds. Simultaneous recordings of spontaneous potential and of the resistivity curve could differentiate impermeable and permeable strata, and hence identify potentially oil-bearing beds.

In 1949 Henri Doll introduced the first induction log, measurements of resistivity after inducing alternating current loops in a formation that made it easier to distinguish oil-bearing rocks from water-bearing substrates. Porous formations that contain only salt water have very low resistivities (often less than 10 Ω) and those that might harbor hydrocarbons have high readings (> 50 Ω). Well logging became an indispensable tool for appraising the probabilities of oil discovery, and Schlumberger has retained global leadership in the field by continued introduction of improved devices and by acquisitions of allied companies.

Modern logging uses slim (no wider than twenty five cm), long (six to twenty five m) pipes to house the instruments; these tools are lowered into a new borehole on a flexible electric cable (wireline) spooled out from a special truck and transmit the readings to the surface.

Gamma-ray logs record the natural emissions from radioisotopes present in the formation, thereby distinguishing between shales and sandstones that have different gamma-ray signatures. Logging of the formation's density is based on the decline of gamma ray flux between a source of radiation and detector; in porous rocks more of the emitted rays reach the counter than in dense

> ## WELL LOGGING (*cont.*)
>
> formations. Neutron logging is used to evaluate formation poros-
> ity by measuring its effect on fast neutrons emitted by a source.
> Logging is normally done after a well is drilled but logging-while-
> drilling is now also possible thanks to making various sensors
> (monitoring well inclination, pressure, resistivity, density and
> porosity) part of an integrated bottomhole assembly. Logging-
> while-drilling is particularly useful where using the standard
> wireline tools is difficult or outright impossible (particularly in
> highly deviated wells).

physical variables in or around a well and recording them for
subsequent evaluation.

Despite impressive advances in geophysics, seismic surveys
and computerized data processing and imaging, modern oil
exploration cannot eliminate the risk of drilling dry holes.
And this risk is uncommonly expensive, with deeper drilling on
land and deep offshore wells, a dry hole can cost upwards of
$15–20 million (leasing an offshore rig can easily run at $500,000
a day). Unlike in many other industrial endeavors, nothing
can be salvaged of a miss, although the cost of the failed enterprise can be written off as a business expense (in the US, in full
in the same year). At the same time, oil exploration remains
(despite the reduced probabilities of discovering supergiant or
giant fields) a highly rewarding enterprise. With an average
price of $50/b the discovery of the smallest giant oilfield
(containing half a billion barrels of recoverable crude) represents
a find worth $25 billion, and a smaller field with an ultimately
recoverable volume of 20 Mb would be worth at least one
billion dollars.

By the end of 2006 about 270 seismic crews were exploring
for oil worldwide, with one quarter of these crews working in

the US (demonstrating that investors see considerable prospects even in some of the world's oldest oil provinces), followed by Africa (18%) and the countries of the former USSR and the Far East (each with about 15%). By 2005 the world's most intensively explored oil provinces included all basins in 48 coterminous US states, in Alberta and Saskatchewan, the North Sea and European Russia. Coastal Venezuela, south-western Iran and the seas off north-western Australia belong to oil basins explored with moderate intensity. Partially explored regions include the shelves of West Africa, parts of the Mediterranean and northern China. Essentially unexplored regions with considerable oil production potential include parts of eastern Siberia, large areas off the east coast of Latin America, West Africa and Greenland, and large expanses of Arctic and Antarctic waters (and, of course, Antarctica itself).

Not surprisingly, exploratory drilling activity is greatly stimulated by higher oil prices while their precipitous retreat can lead to drastic retrenchments. US statistics illustrate these fluctuations. In the early 1970s, before OPEC's rapid price rise in 1974, slightly more than 1,000 rotary rigs were searching for oil and gas on land and offshore; the subsequent price rise pushed their total to more than 4,500 by the end of 1981 but by 1985 the count was below 2,000 and by the middle of 1986 (in the wake of the price collapse) it was below 700. Subsequently the total stayed mostly below, or just above 1,000 until a slight rebound that began in 2004, and by the end of 2006 the total was above 1,700, but only 278 rigs (16% of the total) were drilling for oil. And there is always the risk that by the time a well-considered decision to drill is made (after becoming convinced that high oil prices are more than an ephemeral phenomenon) an unforeseeable event, or a foreseeable reversal taking place much sooner than anticipated, can turn a cautious and a highly promising investment into an instant and completely irretrievable loss.

Oil drilling

Regardless of whether the drilling was done in order to explore for oil or to develop newly discovered oilfields and then to maintain and enhance their production, there have been only two dominant techniques used to complete the vast majority of wells since the beginning of the oil era during the 1850s, percussion (cable-tool) drilling during the first half of this period, and rotary drilling afterwards. Remarkably, the technique that was used to sink the first wells explicitly drilled in search of oil has its origin in an ancient Chinese invention. Percussion drilling was used from at least the beginning of the Han dynasty (Rome's great contemporary, constituted about 200 BCE) to extract natural gas in Sichuan province (see figure 13).

Figure 13 Qing dynasty drawing of the ancient Chinese technique of percussion drilling using a bamboo derrick.

The gas was then transported by bamboo pipes and burned under large cast iron pans to evaporate brines and produce salt, a precious commodity in the landlocked province. The method required a congruence of several important technical skills: availability of heavy iron bits and long bamboo poles, manufacturing of strong and long cables woven from bamboo fiber, and a clever use of levers. Heavy iron bits were attached to long bamboo cables that were suspended from bamboo derricks and they were then repeatedly (and rhythmically) raised and dropped into a manually dug hole by two to six men jumping on a lever. This seemingly primitive way of drilling was actually quite effective and its performance improved with use. Han dynasty boreholes made by percussion drilling were only about 10 m deep but by the tenth century wells deeper than 100 m were common and in 1835 the deepest well reached 1 km below the surface! Until 1895 a modernized variant of this ancient Chinese technique was used to drill all new oil wells. Starting with Edwin Drake's first Pennsylvania well in 1859, small steam engines, rather than human muscles, powered the drilling process and heavy metal bits were hung from manila ropes and, later, from multiple-strand steel wires supported by small wooden derricks. Steam power and better bits speeded up the fracturing and pulverization of the drilled substrate but the bailing out of the cuttings accumulated at the bottom of the hole remained laborious. However, the technique remained in use for decades after the introduction of a superior drilling method: cable tool rigs outnumbered rotary drills until 1951.

The first rotary drilling rig was used in the Corsicana field in Texas in 1895, but in the US the technique became significant only with the completion of the record-flowing (up to 80,000 bpd) Spindletop well in Texas in 1901, and it became dominant worldwide only after 1950. The fundamental importance of rotary drilling for both discovering oil and producing it from commercial wells justifies more than a cursory description of its main components and operating procedures. The entire assembly of structures and machines used in rotary drilling is called a rig and its hardware consists of six interconnected systems: power generation, hoisting mechanism, rotary table that turns the drilling pipes and the drilling bit, fluid circulation, blowout prevention and monitoring and well bore data acquisition.

Rigs are visible from afar thanks to their tall, pyramidal derricks, the steel structure that supports the crown block, and the drillstring (see figure 14). The crown block is a combination of fixed pulleys (sheaves) and travelling blocks used to gain a large mechanical advantage to hoist heavy loads with a small-diameter (1.9–3.75 cm) steel cable; the draw works reel the cable over the crown block and thus lower (by gravity) or raise (by electric motors or diesel engines) the travelling block and the load suspended from it, be it drillstring, well casing or well liners. The drillstring is a combination of the drillpipe and attached bottomhole assembly with a drill bit. Other key parts of a rig are the tanks holding the drilling fluids and the pumps to dispense it, engines to power the rig and, of course, the component that gives the technique its specific adjective, the rotary table.

This table is a heavy circular steel section of the drillfloor near the base of a derrick that powers the clockwise (when viewed from above) motion of a drillstring. Early rotaries (and other rig equipment) were energized (via gears) by steam engines. Large diesel engines are now the dominant prime movers and they deliver their torque directly (via drive chains and belts) or they are used first to drive electricity generators and the rigs are then driven by electric motors. The table's clockwise rotation ('turning to the right' in drilling parlance) is transmitted to the drillstring via a kelly bushing and a kelly, a long hollow steel bar with either a square or hexagonal profile.

Drillpipe is a section of tubular steel with threaded ends (tool joints) whose length and diameters vary depending on the

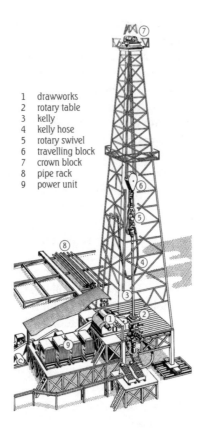

1 drawworks
2 rotary table
3 kelly
4 kelly hose
5 rotary swivel
6 travelling block
7 crown block
8 pipe rack
9 power unit

Figure 14 Modern rotary drilling rig (courtesy of BP).

requirements of a particular job; standard length is 9 m (thirty feet) with an outside diameter of 13.75 cm (5.5 in) and inside diameter of 8.125 cm (3.25 in). Its first segment is attached to a kelly and as the drilling proceeds and a well deepens new sections of threaded drillpipes are connected to a lengthening drillstring which serves as a conduit for drilling fluid. To do so the drilling must stop, the kelly must be disconnected from the top joint and a new section of drill pipe must be mated to the top of the drillstring and to the bottom of the kelly. The rate of penetration (typically in the order of 100 m a day) will determine the number of new connections that can be made in an hour or a day.

The bottomhole assembly attached to the lowermost portion of the drillstring consists of a bit, crossovers for various thread-forms and heavy drill collars to keep the entire rotating assembly vertical. The cost of these assemblies ranges from about $100,000 for the simplest arrangement to more than a million dollars for complex units that contain mud motors that are powered by the drilling fluid and used in directional and horizontal drilling. As a drilling bit wears out the entire drill-string has to be withdrawn from the well, pipe sections have to be unscrewed, stacked aside and then reattached after a new bit is mounted. This process (called tripping) is laborious and dangerous, as heavy pipes are removed, added and manhandled within the limited work area of a rig floor. The earliest rotary drills used fishtails and circular-toothed bits that were effective only in soft rocks. The invention of the rotary cone drill changed that dramatically.

Roller cone bits have either milled teeth or carbide tungsten inserts with embedded industrial diamonds (used in oil drilling for the first time in 1919) whose superior hardness gouges out the rock as the bit rotates. Diamonds are also used in drag bits that have no roller bearings and shear the rock with a continuous scraping motion. Polycrystalline diamond cutters use thin (about 3 mm) circular bits (up to 2.5 cm in diameter) of synthetic diamonds bonded to the underlying tungsten carbide and are preferred for drilling shale formations. Diamond matrix drag bits are used in extremely hard formations. Only about 20%

HISTORY OF ROTARY CONE DRILLS

In 1901 Howard Robard Hughes, who had failed to finish law school and had been working in ore mining, was so impressed by the discovery of the Spindletop oilfield that he switched to oil drilling in Texas. In 1907 he was unable to penetrate extremely hard rock in two promising localities and this failure made him determined to design a better drilling bit – and he did so during just two weeks in November 1908 while visiting his parents in Iowa. His truly revolutionary design was a rotary cone drill (see figure 15) that consisted of two (citing one of the most consequential patents of the twentieth century, granted on 10 August 1909) "frusto-conical shaped rollers having longitudinally extending chisel teeth that disintegrate or pulverize the material with which they come in contact and thus form a round hole in said material when the head of the drill revolves."

The two rollers were arranged at an angle to each other as they rotated on stationary spindles and, of course, as the entire bit rotated at the end of the drillstring. This simple, elegant and near-perfect design made it possible to drill ten times faster than with

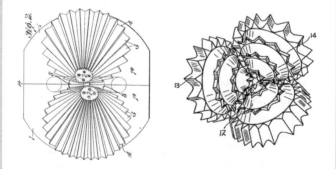

Figure 15 Drawing of the first conical drilling bit in Howard Hughes's 1908 patent application (left), and the first three-cone bit devised in 1933 by Floyd L. Scott and Lewis E. Garfield of the Hughes Tool Company.

HISTORY OF ROTARY CONE DRILLS (*cont.*)

standard fishtail bits. In 1909 Hughes went into partnership with Walter B. Sharp to set up the Sharp-Hughes Tool Company (after 1918 just Hughes Tool) that made the bits, not for sale but for lease, at $30,000 per well. The company used its rising profits well as its engineers kept on improving the basic Hughes tool and developed new modifications. These included a design that was thought to be impossible: in 1933 Floyd L. Scott and Lewis E. Garfield patented a tricone bit, interfitting the cutters of three rotating drill cone bits (see figure 15). This arrangement sped up the drilling, offered a much better support on the well bottom than did the two-cone tool and reduced vibration. Numerous variants still dominate the oil drilling market and the Hughes Company (now Hughes Christensen, part of Baker Hughes) is still their leading producer, with about 30% of the worldwide market share.

of diamonds are sold to the jewellery trade, most of the rest goes into drilling for hydrocarbons and metallic ores.

Besides the kind and the quality of the drilling bit the other key variable that controls the rate of penetration through the drilled rock is the weight on the bit, that is, the mass of the drill-string. Every combination of the bottom hole assembly and the drilled rock has the optimum weight on the bit that will produce the highest rate of penetration: this total is typically between 6.5–9 t. Because the single standard drill pipe weighs about 190 kg this optimum is achieved with only 34–47 sections, that is with total drill string length as short as 300 m. Here is the reason for the already described large mechanical advantage afforded by the wire led over the crown block at the top of the derrick and travelling blocks to the draw works: this arrangement keeps the bit weight at the level commensurate with the fastest rate of penetration by suspending the remaining mass of the drill string. Depending on the number of loops between the two blocks the suspended load can be easily 500 t, enough to support more than 2,000 standard pipe lengths that would reach more than 20 km below the surface, much farther than even the deepest experimental well ever drilled (most oil wells do not go deeper than 4 km).

Rock cuttings produced by an advancing drilling bit are removed from the borehole by a drilling fluid, commonly called drilling mud. This term is a collective label for what has become an enormous variety of liquids and mixtures of liquids, solids and gases. The simplest way to sort out their confusing variety is to classify them into water-based, oil-based, gaseous and synthetic fluids. Water-based muds are natural mixtures or fluids to which lignosulfonates, phosphates, lignite or tannins are added to act as deflocculants and viscosity and filtrate reducers; various emulsifiers, defoamers, polymers, salts, corrosion inhibitors and weighting materials (barite, iron oxide) are also used to control downhole pressure and prevent cave-ins. Oil-based muds are pumped into high-temperature wells or into deep holes where sticking and hole stabilization may be a problem. Synthetic fluids are primarily composed of esters, ethers and olefins. What started simply as the use of water to remove rock cuttings has evolved into a complex industry dealing with scores of varieties of drilling fluids, some of them worth up to \$400/b.

Drilling fluid is pumped under high pressure from a storage container through a rigid metal standpipe that reaches about one-third of the way up the derrick into a kelly hose, a flexible high-pressure conduit (typically 7.5–12.5 cm inside diameter) that is connected to the swivel. The swivel must be strong enough to suspend the weight of the entire drill string and it also allows the flow of pressurized drilling fluid from the flexible hose to a rotating kelly. Drilling mud is forced at high pressure down the kelly into the drill string and eventually it flows through the bit. This constant flow cools the rotating bit, makes the removal of cuttings a continuous and easy operation, and the pressure it puts on the well sides helps to prevent the hole from caving in. The mud loaded with drilling debris returns to the surface through the annulus, the space between the outer drill string wall and the wall of the well bore.

Heavy drill collars are used to add weight and rigidity to the drill string in order to keep the borehole straight and stabilizers may be used at intervals along the string to improve rigidity and to prevent deviation from the vertical. Wells will commonly encounter strata saturated with water, oil or gases or layers of unconsolidated sediments that must be isolated from the progressing borehole (and from each other) by the installation of steel casing that must be fastened in place. Cement was used to do this even in some pre-1900 wells drilled by cable tools, but the first machine that eliminated laborious hand mixing at the drill site and the process that made the cementing of well casing into a routine operation came only in the 1920s.

As in the Schlumberger case, the company that pioneered and commercialized a much improved version of this important operation has retained its primacy ever since the 1920s. In 1919 Erle P. Halliburton started his oil well cementing company in Oklahoma and in 1922 he filed a patent for his new cement jet mixer. Eventually Halliburton expanded into one of the world's largest oilfield service companies (providing not only cementing but also logging and well completion services as well as drill bits) and because of its merger with Dresser (another major energy industry provider) and the acquisition of Brown & Root (builders of the first offshore oil platform in 1947 and a large general contractor) it is now also one of the world's leading multifunctional engineering enterprises.

As the exploratory wells deepened and began encountering higher reservoir pressures it became imperative to devise new means of preventing well kicks and blowouts during drilling, tripping or when the drill string is out of the well bore. A kick takes place anytime the pressure in the well bore becomes lower than the pressure of the surrounding formation fluids. Kicks are caused either by insufficient mud weight, be it because of initial low mud density or its lowering by an inflow of lighter liquids or gases (an underbalanced kick), or because of sudden pressure changes caused by the movement of the drill string or casing (an induced kick).

Violent blowouts not only eject the drill pipe from the borehole but lead to fires that can kill crew members and destroy a rig. The first blowout preventer, designed by James S. Abercrombie and Harry S. Cameron in 1922 could contain formation pressures of up to 20 MPa in 20 cm diameter holes; in contrast, some of today's high-performance preventers used to drill in geopressured zones can contain formation pressures up to 100 MPa in boreholes with diameters up to 46 cm. Blowout preventers must be able to shut the well at the surface by using various ramming devices, rid the well bore of the unwanted fluid and replace it with a heavier fluid that will prevent future intrusions. Ever since these devices have been widely deployed accidental blowouts have become increasingly rare. New measures and procedures were also put in place to minimize the damage of an inadvertent blowout and to allow for a safe and rapid evacuation of drilling rigs, precautions that are particularly critical in offshore oil drilling.

Myron Kinley put out the first well blowout with explosives in 1913 and a decade later he set up the first company to control wild wells. Kinley trained Paul Neal Adair, who formed the Red Adair Company in 1959 and became the most famous of all oil well fire fighters, as well as Asger Hansen and Edward O. Matthews, who, in turn, left Adair's company in 1978 to set up another famous well control outfit, Boots and Coots. In 1997 International Well Control (formed after Adair's retirement and the sale of his company) acquired Boots and Coots and reunited the top expertise in fast control and safe capping of runaway wells. Safety Boss in Calgary is another well control company operating globally. Extinguishing more than 700 oil wells set on fire in Kuwait in March 1991 by the retreating Iraqi army was the biggest ever test of these dangerous skills.

Despite a high level of mechanization the operation of modern oil drilling rigs still requires a great deal of heavy (and often) dangerous labor during which most of the crew (now typically about twenty workers per land rig) is exposed to weather. The lowest ranking members of a drilling crew are roustabouts who do all unskilled peripheral manual jobs ranging from offloading and moving the drilling supplies, stacking drill pipes and mixing drilling fluids to cleaning, scraping and painting the deck. Roughnecks handle all the manual tasks of the drilling operation, adding new lengths of drill pipe, disassembling the drill string prior to changing the drill bit or retrieving core samples and cleaning all drilling equipment. Skilled jobs are those of motormen, derrickmen, assistant drillers, and the driller who supervises the entire crew and operates the pumps, draw works and rotary table from a console in his control room. Drilling usually proceeds round the clock, requiring two or three shifts on land and two twelve-hour shifts offshore.

Better drills and faster drilling operations combined with the need to search for oil in deeper reservoirs led to a steady increase of both record and average drilling depths. Record US well depths reached with rotary rigs increased from 300 m in 1895 to more than 1.5 km by 1916; the 3 km mark was reached in 1930, the deepest pre-WWII well was 4.5 km (in 1938) and the 6 km mark was surpassed in 1950. Beyond this the drilling entered the ultradeep range where high temperatures, high pressures and often a highly corrosive environment, present new challenges. Many of these wells were drilled in Oklahoma's Anadarko basin where the 9 km barrier was passed in 1974. The average depth of new US wells drilled in 2005 in the search for oil was about 4.3 km, and that of development wells in producing oilfields only about 1.6 km.

The two most notable post-WWII advances in oil drilling were the move into deeper offshore waters, and the development of directional drilling. Offshore drilling uses the same tools and procedures as operations on land but it faces major technical challenges in positioning the drilling platforms. For decades offshore drilling was just a simple extension of onshore operations. The first drilling from wooden wharves extending short distances from the shore was done in California as early as 1897. The first permanent wooden production platforms were built in the shallow waters of Lake Maracaibo in 1924, by 1927 concrete pilings were providing better anchoring, and in 1934 came the first standardized steel platforms whose numbers eventually multiplied to dot the lake with tall metal structures.

The first near-shore well was drilled in the Gulf of Mexico in 1937 and by the mid-1940s Texas prospectors had rigs drilling from submersible barges. Baku's oil is only partly onshore and hence from the earliest days of its exploitation efforts were made to find the best solutions for drilling offshore. Between 1909 and 1932 Bibi-Heybat Bay was filled with earth in order to drill offshore deposits; in 1924 a small woodpile island was built in Bayil Limani and in 1949 drilling began from a large steel offshore pier at Neft Dashlari. In 1947 the first oil well (Kermac 16) drilled out of sight of land (nearly 70 km from the Louisiana shore) was completed in 6 m of water by Kerr-McGee Corporation in the Gulf of Mexico. Offshore drilling diffused from the Gulf of Mexico to California, to the further reaches of Lake Maracaibo and to Brazil's coastal waters and it progressed from small submersible units suitable only for shallow waters to a variety of drill ships and semisubmersible rigs designed for year-round drilling even in such stormy waters as the North Sea.

In all old oil provinces there are many shallow oil-bearing formations that were bypassed during the original development (that sought more substantial reservoirs). Short-radius (less than 20 m) drilling to produce horizontal laterals from thousands of

OFFSHORE DRILLING

In 1949 John Hayward combined a submersible barge and a piled platform to build the first submersible rig, *Breton Rig 20*; he devised a way to stabilize a ballasted barge on the seafloor so that only the columns (connected to the barge and supporting the rig's working deck) were exposed to waves. Kerr-McGee bought the rig in 1950, after it had drilled nineteen wells. A better version, *Mr. Charlie*, was built in 1953 by Alden J. Laborde who founded the Ocean Drilling & Exploration Company (ODECO). That company eventually combined with three other pioneers of marine drilling to form Transocean, the world's leader in offshore engineering.

The first self-elevating (jack-up) drilling rig, *Offshore Rig 51*, began working in 1954. Its ten legs (1.8 m in diameter and 48 m long) ended in large spud cans to minimize the pressure of the ocean floor. A prototype of modern jack-ups – a triangular platform with three legs and pinions driven by electric motors – was built by Le Tourneau Company in 1956. Jack-ups were not suitable for deeper waters and in 1961 Shell Oil was the first company to deploy a semisubmersible rig, *Bluewater I*, in the Gulf of Mexico. Different designs followed in rapid succession – and a decade after the first model there were thirty semisubmersibles at work.

During the 1970s Transocean introduced the *Discoverer*-class drill ships whose operations proceeded to set repeated drilling records: by the year 2000 the fifth generation of these ships could drill in waters 3 km deep. By the end of 2006, there were roughly 650 mobile offshore rigs deployed worldwide, with more than 20% of them in US waters.

A new chapter of offshore drilling began with operations in very deep water. The industry defines work at a depth of 1,500 m (5,000 ft) as ultra-deep drilling, and the Gulf of Mexico has the world's highest concentration of such projects and associated records, including an exploratory well drilled in 2003 by *Discoverer Deep Seas* in more than 3,000 m of water. In 2004 there were twelve rigs drilling in the Gulf's waters, five of them in depths of more than 2 km.

OFFSHORE DRILLING (*cont.*)

These efforts have been rewarded with regular new major deepwater finds, six in 2003, eight in 2004, and nine in 2005. On September 5, 2006 a consortium of Chevron, Devon Energy and Statoil announced some details of their record-setting explorations in the Gulf of Mexico. Their *Jack 2* well was set 280 km offshore in water about 2.1 km deep and then penetrated more than 6 km before encountering oil at a total drilling depth of 8.45 km. And this was no ordinary discovery: preliminary estimates credited the field with reserves of anywhere between 3–25 Gb, clearly a giant field and, if the higher total is verified, the largest discovery since the Alaskan Prudhoe Bay in 1968 and an impressive supergiant.

abandoned and existing wells could add to production without any new surface disturbance. They could also have cables or fiber optic links embedded in their walls allowing for an unprecedented degree of logging while drilling, creating a smart drill pipe. Research is now underway to develop a composite drill pipe (CDP) whose cost could be competitive with traditional steel tube. Major challenges include not only the cost of CDP production but also difficulties in interfacing between the composite material and steel joints and in developing suitable coatings (composites are much less wear and abrasion resistant than steel).

Early drillers sank many wells that deviated significantly from the vertical; after all, a deviation of just 10° will take a well nearly 500 m off the vertical at a depth of 3 km. As a result, boreholes in early oilfields tapped unintentionally into neighboring drilling claims, sometimes they even merged with another well. The significance of this unintentional deviation from the vertical axis was recognized as a problem for the first time during the mid-1920s in Oklahoma and it led eventually to the development of directional drilling (deviating by increasingly greater angles from the vertical) and then true horizontal drilling and extended reach drilling (where horizontal components are at least twice as long as the vertical bore).

The first short horizontal wells were drilled in 1929 in Texas and in 1937 in the USSR, and John Eastman and John Zublin designed and used the first short-radius (6–9 m) drilling tools in California during the early 1940s. These trials confirmed the feasibility of this new technique but its high costs did not justify commercial adoption and it was only during the late 1970s that interest in horizontal drilling was rekindled both in North America and in Europe and during the 1980s when the process became a commercial success. During the 1980s North American hydrocarbon companies drilled more than 300 horizontal wells (mostly with a medium-radius of around 30 m), but ten times as many were completed during the 1990s.

As the technique advanced the returns became impressive: a horizontal well can be two or three times more expensive than a vertical well of the same length (mostly because of problems with high torque and drag while drilling, and with the well bore's integrity) but through its superior penetration of an oil-bearing formation it can enhance production by as much as fifteen or twenty-fold. Initial doubts about not being able to drill beyond 70° inclination were soon dispelled with successful 90° wells. Small deviations can be effected by using different weights on a bit or by varying drill speed. Greater departures from the vertical were obtained by placing inclined hard steel wedges (whipstocks) on the bottom of a borehole (or on top of a tempo-rary cement plug), forcing the drill bit to deviate in the desired direction; obviously, this allowed only limited directional control and led to many missed targets.

The solution was to harness the kinetic energy of the drilling fluid to power the drilling bits. By the mid-1950s turbine drilling was converting the hydraulic power of the drilling mud into rotary power turning the bit, but today's positive displacement motors deployed in directional drilling are reverse applications of Rene Moineau's concept of an irrigation pump that could tolerate a high influx of solids. Unlike the turbines with hundreds of rotor-stator power section stages, modern drilling motors have a small number of stator and rotor lobes ranging from single-lobe (one rotor) designs to motors with nine rotors and ten stators. Rotors are placed eccentrically and their motion about the stator axis acts as a gear reduction that lowers the speed and increases the torque as the number of lobes increases.

Positive displacement motors are powered by the pressurized drilling fluid (and consequently called mud motors) that is commonly delivered at rates of 350–600 liters per minute, their rotation is restricted to standard speeds of 200–250 rpm, and the latest designs have power output as high as 400 kW. These motors are used to point the bit away from the vertical axis when the drill string is not rotating and to drill in a new, non-vertical direction; once this new direction is well established it can be maintained by rotating the entire drill string, including the bent section. This is an inefficient arrangement (as extreme torque and drag restrict the drilling capability), and one that also produces an uneven (overgauge and spiral) borehole that may cause difficulties for logging and casing operations. These problems were eliminated by the introduction of rotary steerable drilling motors during the mid-1990s.

The latest models integrate a high-power drilling motor with continuous drill string rotation. The drill string rotates only at a speed sufficient to agitate and to remove the cuttings and its continuous motion also transfers weight to the bit more efficiently. But the drill string's rate of rotation is decoupled from that of a high-speed drill (powered by a mud motor via gearing) whose steering and control are energized from a power-generating module (a turbine-driven alternator) in the bottom-hole assembly. This arrangement keeps the well bore clean, it produces a smooth and in-gauge borehole and it allows for a high rate of penetration. Steerable downhole motors are also used in coiled tubing drilling, introduced during the late 1990s. This method has replaced standard rigid steel pipes with narrow (2.5–11.25 cm in diameter) flexible steel tubing that is wrapped on a large spool mounted on a heavy trailer and straightened before it is unreeled into a well bore. Overall lengths of continuous coiled tubing range from about 600 m for the largest to about 4,500 m for the smallest diameter. Slim-hole drilling eliminates the laborious tripping, and new high speed turbine drills (with up to 10,000 rpm) produce very high rates of penetration.

The benefits of directional drilling are obvious: for example, if the oil-bearing strata are 3 km below the surface then drilling at 70° rather than at 60° angle off the vertical will make it possible to reach an area that is nearly 2.5 times larger from the same drilling site. The most extreme case of directional drilling is following a near-horizontal (in excess of 80°) or a perfectly horizontal direction, or even an undulating pattern along it (see figure 16). Such wells have boosted recovery rates as they can be directed through relatively thin oil-bearing strata that would be uneconomical to drill with a series of vertical wells. The world's longest extended reach well – BP's Wytch Farm M11 in Dorset, completed in 1998 in just 173 days after reaching 10,658 m (vertically only 1,605 m) to tap deposits under Poole Bay – is far longer than the deepest commercial vertical well. And horizontal wells open new production prospects in sandy reservoirs and in formations with water or gas problems or low permeability.

The US has a rigorous system for reporting the finding costs of oil and gas measured on a combined basis in barrels of oil equivalent (boe) and these data reveal significant differences between onshore and offshore operations, the relatively high cost of US and Canadian discoveries and some interesting secular trends. During 2003–2005 the cost of land discoveries in

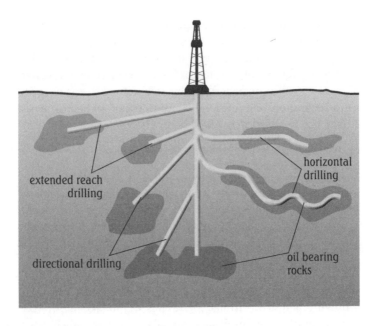

Figure 16 Directional and horizontal drilling.

the US averaged $6.67/boe, compared to about $10/boe in 2001, and only about a third of the average finding costs during the early 1980s. In contrast, drilling in the deep water of the Gulf of Mexico has led to exponentially rising costs in finding offshore oil, from about $10/boe in 2001 to nearly $28/boe in 2002–2004 and almost $43/boe in 2003–2005. Still, the combined cost of US discoveries, $9.79/boe in 2003–2005, is only about half of the total that prevailed in the early 1980s.

The recent Canadian rate has been more than twice as high as the US mean, but oil companies had to spend about 35% less to discover a barrel of oil in the Middle East than they did in the US. Worldwide, the average cost of finding new oil was about $9/boe in 2002–2004, about 25% up when compared to 2000, nearly twice as high as in the early 1990s but only half as high as in the early 1980s; it must be stressed that all of these figures reflect only the finding costs of companies that are legally required to provide information to the US Financial Reporting System and that finding costs are definitely lower for many national companies in OPEC countries.

History of oil discoveries

Many societies have known about hydrocarbons from seepages, bitumen pools and burning pillars, particularly encountered throughout the Middle East. But, unlike in the case of metallic ores, there were no attempts to discover underground oil deposits because the exploitation of heavier hydrocarbons was limited to a few (and localized) uses. Some ancient Mesopotamian cultures used asphalts and bitumens to inlay floor and wall mosaics and for protective coatings and burned lighter oils in fire pans for illumination. So did, centuries later, the Romans in some Asian localities (who, following the Greek example, also used oil as a charge for flaming containers during sieges and naval battles) and then various peoples of the Byzantine Empire, Muslim caliphates and the Ottoman Empire. Oil was also known in pre-industrial France: oil shales were mined during the first half of the eighteenth century in Pechelbronn in Alsace (oil, sold in small bottles, was reputed to be a miraculous remedy).

The place with the longest tradition of local crude oil use (as well as small-scale exports) is undoubtedly the Absheron peninsula of the Baku region on the Caspian Sea in Azerbaijan. Absheron's oil pools and wells were described by medieval Arabic travelers and historians, a 35 m deep hand-dug well in Balakhani had an inscription dating it to 1593, and by the late eighteenth century there were scores of shallow wells from which oil (particularly the 'white' variety) was extracted for the production of kerosene (by primitive thermal distillation) for local lighting as well as for export (in skins) by camels and ships. In 1837 Russians (Baku became a part of the czarist empire in 1806) set up the first commercial oil-distilling factory in Balakhani and in 1846 the world's first exploratory oil well was drilled to the depth of 21 m in Bibi-Heybat.

During the 1850s the rising cost of whale oil used for illumination led a number of entrepreneurs to search for alternatives and to the small-scale beginnings of new oil-based industries. In 1853 Abraham Gesner began to produce kerosene from coal in his North American Kerosene Gas and Lighting Company on Long Island. Ignacy Lukasiewicz, a Polish pharmacist, followed Gesner's work and became the first chemist to distill kerosene from oil found in seeps near Krosno where he opened an oil mine in 1854 and two years later the first distillery. America's first oil well was hand-dug near Black Creek hamlet in a swamp in Lambton County in south-western Ontario in 1858 by Charles Tripp and James Miller Williams. Extraction was by buckets dipped into the well and emptied into barrels which were then transported for primitive refining in large, wood-heated, cauldrons to yield kerosene and the residual lubricating grease. By 1859 the area was experiencing the world's first oil rush as burgeoning Black Creek was renamed Oil Springs.

In the same year came the first US oil rush. Oil seeps in western Pennsylvania were known by the Seneca tribe and during the eighteenth century bottled 'Seneca oil' was sold as a medicine. George Bissell, a New York lawyer, set up the Pennsylvania Rock Oil Company (later Seneca Oil) after Benjamin Silliman at Yale (hired by Bissell) confirmed that oil's distillation yields kerosene. In 1859 Edwin Drake (sent by Bissell to start regular production at Oil Creek near Titusville, Pennsylvania) hired a local blacksmith to find the source of the largest seep by drilling the first US oil well. After a slow progress of about 1 m a day the well struck oil (extracted by a hand-operated pump) at the depth of 21 m on 27 August 1859. The well initially yielded twenty-five barrels a day, but by the year's end the flow was down to fifteen barrels.

With the market limited largely to lighting kerosene and lubricants the growth of new oil discoveries was relatively slow during the closing decades of the nineteenth century. The Canadian oil boom intensified in 1862 when Hugh Nixon Shaw, going against the prevailing wisdom that no oil would be found at depths below 20 m, produced the world's first gusher from the depth of 60 m, but soon the reservoir pressure began to decline and the Oil Springs wells had to use steam pumps. A second oil rush came with new discoveries at Petrolea (soon renamed Petrolia), about 15 km north of Oil Springs, in 1865, but the Ontario oil boom was over by 1891 when John D. Rockefeller's Standard Oil Company flooded the market with cheaper American oil. The company was set up in 1870 and within a decade it controlled about 80% of the market for kerosene and other refined products.

In 1875 Ludwig and Robert Nobel (Alfred's brothers) launched their Caspian oil enterprise (which eventually became Baku's leading oil-producing enterprise: Nobel Brothers Petroleum Company) and in 1877 they built the world's first oil-carrying steamship, *Zoroaster*. In 1878 an oil gusher at Bibi-Heybat demonstrated the oilfield's exceptional size: the field eventually produced enough crude oil to be classified as the world's first known giant oilfield, that is one with at least 500 million barrels of recoverable crude oil (see figure 17). The Rothschild brothers began investing in Baku in 1883 when they established the Caspian and Black Sea Oil Industry and Trade Society.

The first US giant oilfields were Bradford (1875) and Allegany (1879) in Pennsylvania and Brea-Olinda (1884) and McKittrick (1887) in California. The first oil-producing well in Texas was drilled in 1866 but the first economically important strike was in 1894 in Corsicana, made by a city crew drilling for

Figure 17 A forest of wooden oil derricks in Baku in 1886.

water and in 1895 the area's first producing wells were drilled by Joseph S. Cullinan who later became one of the founders of Texas Company (which became Texaco, in 1901). The most important discovery came on 10 January 1901 when a well drilled by Anthony F. Lucas in Spindletop near Beaumont produced a thirty m tall gusher that took nine days to cap. Another oil boom followed, but Spindletop's enormous output (17.5 million barrels in 1902) brought an oil glut and prices plummeted to three cents a barrel. Other notable pre-WWI oil discoveries were made in Romania, Indonesia, Burma and Iran.

As in the Baku region, pools and shallow wells of oil had been known in southern Romania for centuries, and during the 1840s workshops using simple distillation were built in Lucacesti-Bacau. A true commercial refinery, using cast iron cylinders, began operating in Ploiesti (60 km north of Bucharest) in 1857. The country's only giant oilfield, Moreni–Gura Ocnitei, was discovered in 1900.

Discovery of oil in northern Sumatra in 1883, at that time a part of the Dutch East Indies, led to the establishment of the Koninklijke Nederlandsche Maatschappij tot Exploitatie van Petroleum-bronnen in Nederlandsch Indië (Royal Dutch Company for Exploration of Petroleum sources in the Netherlands Indies) by Jean Baptiste August Kessler, Henri Deterding and Hugo Loudon in 1890. In 1907 the company merged with the Shell Transport and Trading Company set up in 1897 by Marcus and Samuel Samuel (in 1833 their father Marcus established a small shop in London selling seashells, a legacy that created one of the world's most recognizable logos) to form Royal Dutch Shell.

The Burmah Oil Company was set up in Glasgow in 1886 and it began producing oil a year later, with most of its extraction coming from moderately-size fields at Yenangyaung, Chauk and Minbu. Iranian exploration began with the concession granted in May 1901 to William Knox D'Arcy to drill in Ghasr-e-Shirin and Chah-Sorkh. By 1904 D'Arcy had spent what was for that time the enormous sum of £220,000 without striking any commercial oil quantities. His enterprise was rescued in 1905 by new funds provided by the Burmah Oil Company. A new syndicate negotiated a contract (never recognized by the Persian government) with Bahktiari chiefs to drill in the south-west, near the Iraqi border, and on 26 May 1908 came the discovery of the first Middle Eastern oilfield at Masjid-e-Soleiman. In 1909 the Anglo-Persian Oil Company (the precursor of British Petroleum) was set up to develop the field and in 1914 it reached an agreement with the British Admiralty to supply oil for warships being converted from coal to liquid fuel (both the British and the German navy decided on the switch just before WWI) and the government became the company's majority shareholder.

During the early decades of the twentieth century important strikes were made in North Texas, and in October 1930 the state's biggest field, East Texas, was discovered by a wildcatter C.M. Joiner who took up the claim after it was rejected by geologists working for large oil companies as unpromising. Another frenzied boom and another overproduction followed and in August 1931 the field was placed under martial law and the Texas Railroad Commission began to enforce a production quota. East Texas was the largest of the three Texas giants that began production between 1925 and 1950: the other two were Yates, discovered in 1926, and Wasson, in West Texas near the New Mexico border, in 1936. The latter field was exceptionally large (about 25,000 hectares) and by the end of the 1990s its cumulative extraction was surpassed only by the East Texas oilfield.

Exploratory drilling began to expand just before the century's end and in retrospect it is clear that the entire first half of the twentieth century was the golden age of oil discoveries as news of new giant oilfields became commonplace. By 1900 the US had only seven giant oilfields, by 1925 the total had risen to seventy-five, by 1950 the count had risen to 220. Two Californian fields were the largest American oilfields discovered between 1900 and 1925, Midway Sunset in 1901 and Wilmington Trend in 1922. Mexican crude oil production began in 1901 and by 1920 the country was the world's second largest producer, and the top exporter, of crude oil. This position was lost despite the discovery of Poza Rica field near Veracruz in 1932, because of major Venezuelan finds and even more impressive Middle Eastern oil discoveries. The first Venezuelan giant, Mene Grande on Lake Maracaibo's east coast, was discovered in 1914, the supergiant Bolivar Coastal in 1917, and two giants, La Paz and Quiriquire were added during the 1920s.

The first major Middle Eastern strike outside Iran was made by Turkish Petroleum, set up in 1912 to seek concessions from the Ottoman government to drill in Iraq. The deal was finally concluded with a new Iraqi government in 1925 and oil was discovered at Baba Gurgur just north of Kirkūk in October 1927. Production by the (renamed) Iraq Petroleum Company began in 1934 and Kirkūk proved to be a supergiant that produced the bulk of Iraqi oil until the Rumaila field near Basra (discovered in 1953) entered production. In Iran exploration by the Anglo-Iranian Oil Company added giants at Gachsaran and Haft Kel in 1928, Naft-i-Said in 1935, Pazaran in 1937 and Agha Jari a year later.

On 29 May 1933 the most important concession to date to explore for oil was signed in Jiddah by the king 'Abd al-'Azīz (the head of the newly constituted [in September 1932] state of Saudi Arabia). California Arabian Standard Oil Company (CASOC), an affiliate of Standard Oil of California (Socal, today's Chevron) made an initial payment of £35,000 in gold for the rights to prospect for oil in al-Hasa (today's Eastern province). Prospecting began in September 1933 and the first giant oilfield, Dammam on the western shore of the Persian Gulf near Dhahrān, was discovered in 1938. This find was soon followed by discoveries of the nearby (and much larger) Abqaiq and Abu Hadriya and Qatif (just north of Dhahrān). In 1944 CASOC became Arabian American Oil Company (Aramco) and in 1948 the company discovered al-Ghawār south-west of Dhahrān that was, after extensive drilling, confirmed in 1956 to be the world's largest accumulation of crude oil.

During the late 1940s came the discoveries of the first Canadian giants in Alberta, Leduc-Woodland in 1947 and Redwater in 1948. Russia's, and after 1921 the USSR's, oil extraction was dominated by the Caspian oilfields until after WWII. Three giant fields were discovered in the Baku area, Balakhani-Sabunchi-Romani in 1896, Karachukhur-Zykh in 1928 and Neft Dashlari in 1949. After WWII the region between the Volga and Ural rivers rapidly emerged as the country's largest oil province, with giant fields discovered in Tuymazy (in what is now autonomous Bashkortostan) in 1937, Mukhanovo in 1945 and Romashkino (in today's Tatarstan) in 1948.

The enormous post WWII increase in demand (detailed in chapter 1) was easily met by new giant oilfield discoveries during the 1950s and 1960s, mostly in the Middle East. The most remarkable finds of those two decades included the supergiants in the Persian-Zagros oil province. The USSR's center of oil production began its second shift, from the Volga-Ural region to Western Siberia, with the discovery of the supergiant Samotlor (in 1965), and Prudhoe Bay on the North Slope of Alaska (1968) became America's largest supergiant.

Canadian reserves were boosted by giants at Pembina and Weyburn-Midale, Swan Hills and Judy Creek, all found in the 1950s. New entries to the list of countries with major oil reserves included Algeria, Libya and Nigeria. And in 1959 Russian and Chinese geologists discovered the supergiant Daqing oilfield in Heilongjiang; nearly half a century later it is still China's largest oil producer. This was also the period of the first major offshore finds in the relatively shallow waters of the Gulf of Mexico and the Persian Gulf.

During the 1970s – the decade of unprecedented OPEC-driven oil price rises and the ensuing 'energy crises' (see chapter 1 for details) and global economic slow-down, the discoveries of giant oilfields were still (albeit only marginally) ahead of the total for the 1960s, but the total amount of recoverable reserves in these fields was nearly 50% lower: new found giants were getting, on average, noticeably smaller. The biggest addition was Mexico's Cantarell Complex in 1976 that eventually became the world's third largest field in terms of average daily production, and North Sea exploration was finally rewarded with several giant finds, all in Norwegian waters.

After the collapse of high oil prices (in 1985) global hydrocarbon exploration shrank dramatically while the price fluctuated but remained (in inflation-adjusted terms) well below the 1981 peak. Investment in new exploratory activities remained low during the 1990s and it began to rise significantly only with the rise in oil prices in 2005. Nevertheless, the last two decades of the twentieth century brought some notable giant oilfield discoveries; including Norway's Draugen (1984), Heidrun (1985) and Norne (1992), Mexico's Caan and Chuc in 1985 and Sihil in 1999, Iran's supergiant Azadegan (in 1999), Kazakhstan's supergiant Kashgan (2000), Brazil's Marlim (1985), Albacora (1986) and Roncador (1996) and new US giants, Ursa (1991), Auger (1996) and Alpine and Thunder Horse (1999).

But, unmistakably, both the rate of new giant oil discoveries and their average size have been declining, from 110 during the 1970s to fifty during the 1980s and to only about forty during the 1990s, while the total of estimated reserves present in these newly discovered fields declined even faster, from the peak of about 270 Gb during the 1960s to only about 30 Gb during the 1990s (but reserve appreciation will certainly raise the latter total). These are important trends because (as explained in chapter 2) the frequency of the world's oilfield sizes is hyperbolically distributed. Given this distribution of oilfields it is inevitable that the countries with the highest number of giants (or with a few supergiants) are the ones with the largest oil reserves. In 2005 the top ten nations on this list were (with shares of the world's oil reserves, rounded to the nearest 0.5%, in parentheses): Saudi Arabia (22), Iran (11), Iraq (10), Kuwait and the United Arab Emirates (each 8), Venezuela (6.5), Russia (6), Libya and Kazakhstan (each 3.5) and Nigeria (3). The five Persian Gulf countries that head this list thus had nearly 60% of the world's oil reserves (see figure 18). The US reserves were only about 2.5% of the global total in 2005.

Another remarkable fact is the astonishing growth of global oil reserves during the second half of the twentieth century, a progress that has been recorded since 1945 thanks to

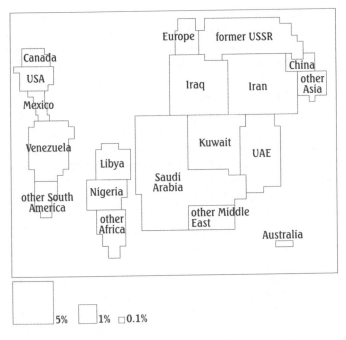

Figure 18 Map of the world with the size of countries and continents proportional to their share of oil reserves in 2005.

the worldwide surveys conducted by two of the oil industry's leading journals, *World Oil* and *Oil & Gas Journal*. A retrospective look using *Oil & Gas Journal* estimates shows the growth of global oil reserves from just 50 Gb in 1945 and 85Gb in 1950 to about 715 Gb by 1974: no other period of twenty-five years has seen, or is ever likely to record, a similarly huge gain. After a decade of stagnation global oil reserves surpassed 900 Gb in 1988, the 1 Tb mark (1.007) was reached in 1995, by the year 2000 the total rose to 1.028 Tb, by 2005 to 1.292 Tb, and as of 1 January 2007 it stood at 1.317 Tb.

GLOBAL R/P RATIO

There is probably no greater testament to the innovative drive of the oil industry and to continuous advances in geophysical surveys and exploratory drilling than the fact that oil companies have been able to find not only enough oil to counter the depletion of reserves and to satisfy the rising demand but that the new discoveries have actually resulted in a secular increase of the global reserve/production (R/P) ratio, a quotient of the latest available reserve estimate and annual oil extraction. The best available data shows this ratio at just over twenty years in 1945. A wave of new (largely Middle Eastern and Russian) discoveries lifted it to forty years by the late 1950s and a subsequent decline brought it to a low of twenty-six years in 1979. By the late 1980s the ratio reached a new record high of nearly forty-five years and at the beginning of 2005 it stood, according to *Oil & Gas Journal*, at forty-four years and according to BP at 40.5 years (see figure19).

These figures illustrate a remarkable achievement as exploration and development were not only able to prevent the global R/P ratio from falling below twenty-five years but were actually able to increase it above forty years despite the nearly twelve-fold rise of

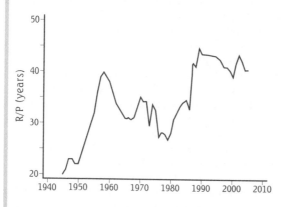

Figure 19 Crude oil's global R/P ratio, 1945–2006.

GLOBAL R/P RATIO (*cont.*)

global oil production between 1945 and 2005. While the overall trend of rising global R/P ratios is real, there are doubts concerning some of the changes in the reported totals of national oil reserves. This concern is due to the absence of rigorous and uniform international standards; as a result, many values are not comparable and some national totals have always been suspect. Proved reserves, the concept used by the US Securities and Exchange Commission (SEC), refer only to the oil that is ready to be produced in the near term. Proved and probable reserves (used in Canada) also count oil where the probability of production over the lifetime of an oilfield is fairly high. And there are estimates of possible reserves for which the probability of eventual extraction cannot be realistically appraised.

This chronic incompatibility problem was overshadowed in 1987 when the record increase in world oil reserves took place not because of any exceptional discoveries (at that time worldwide exploratory activity was actually at its lowest post-1950 level) but because six OPEC members simply announced a massive upward revision of their oil reserves. This upgrade accounted for nearly 90% of the overall 27% jump recorded in global oil reserves in 1987. Iraq and Iran, at that time at war, made the largest revisions of, respectively, 112% and 90%. Upward revaluations of existing reserves are the norm in the oil industry but the magnitude of this increase and its timing (following the collapse of world oil prices) made it suspect. Other suspect totals have remained unchanged for years.

Only the opening of books by national oil companies (an unlikely prospect) would settle the matter. At the same time, oil reserve claims that must be filed with the US Security and Exchange Commissions by all publicly listed oil companies are definitely on the conservative side, and the Russian oil reserves (Russia uses its own resource classification developed during the Soviet era) are almost certainly higher than the published Western estimates. R/P ratios are thus an uncertain (even a misleading) accounting tool and, moreover, one that is subject to deliberate manipulation and hence it should not be used as a dependable indicator of future developments.

4

How oil is produced, transported and processed

The discovery of exploitable amounts of crude oil is only the beginning of a long process of developing a field, managing extraction, transporting and refining the oil and distributing the refined products to their final markets. Proper field management aims at sustaining the longest possible period of production; some currently productive fields are now more than 100 years old.

Once a borehole is drilled to the desired depth the results of logging must be carefully evaluated in order to decide if the well is to be completed, that is, if the borehole will be protected with the heavy steel casing that is cemented in place to create a well, or if it will be abandoned (plugged with cement). Exploration is a success if there are sufficient indications that hydrocarbons are present in commercially recoverable concentrations; in the oil industry's argot, a prospect (also called an anomaly) turns into a play (an area where hydrocarbons are known to be present). But even major finds are not converted immediately into production wells. Their exploitation must await the additional drilling that is required to delineate a field in greater detail, to determine the volume of recoverable oil more accurately and to decide on the best course of the entire field's development. And even then a decision can be made to temporarily shut down the wells if falling oil prices turn the development of a new and relatively expensive oilfield into a marginal proposition. On the other hand, old shut-down marginal wells that require expensive pumping may be reopened if world oil prices rise.

The high concentration of oil production in a handful of the largest oil provinces and the rising worldwide consumption of liquid fuels had to be bridged by the emergence of large-scale transport and storage techniques. Worldwide shipments of crude oils and refined oil products (over long distances by pipelines and tankers, on shorter distances by railway tank cars and trucks) add up to the single largest transfer of a mass-produced mineral commodity on Earth.

Crude oil is such a complex mixture of organic compounds that its direct combustion would represent an enormous waste of a valuable non-renewable resource. Separating the mixture into several principal categories with a more homogeneous composition (but still of considerable heterogeneity) adds a great deal of value to the final products that can be marketed for specific uses at prices commensurate to their relative scarcity and overall utility. This process of separating crude oil into specific fuels (and non-fuel products) is done by refining, that is by subjecting crude oil to a variety of physical and chemical treatments designed to maximize the yield of the desired final products.

Oil production

Success in exploration leads to more drilling before a reservoir is developed for commercial production. More wells are sunk in order to delineate a reservoir's extent and depth and to emplace production wells in order to optimize long-term extraction. During the subsequent decades new wells are drilled to monitor, maintain and to enhance production (surveillance and injection wells). As oilfields age and reservoir pressure drops new wells are sunk in order to tap previously unexploited parts of a formation, to enhance oil recovery by introducing fluids into oil-bearing strata through special injection wells, or to store gas. Old boreholes are re-entered to deepen the existing wells and both active and abandoned boreholes can be used as new entries for horizontal or multilateral drilling. Development wells are thus much more numerous than exploratory ones, and well completion aims at ensuring that oil can keep flowing into a well and that it can be reliably brought to the surface while water (be it above or below the oil-bearing strata) and the rock formation surrounding the well are kept out.

Modern wells are completed with steel casing extending over the entire oil-bearing zone (the casing is run all the way to the well's bottom where it is cemented in place) and hence it is necessary to ensure that oil will flow into the well from the surrounding formation. Various mechanical methods have been used to puncture holes in the casing, including firing special bullets from short-barrel guns. The standard practice today is to use shaped charges whose high-velocity detonation easily penetrates the well's steel casing and the surrounding cement and blasts short narrow holes into the oil-bearing rocks, allowing the free flow of hydrocarbons into the well. Perforations can be made in precisely placed spots along the casing in order to minimize the ingress of unwanted fluids (above all, salty formation water).

Most of the oil produced from deep wells is drawn through tubing, a special string of pipes inside the casing. The principal reason for this practice is the ease of repairs: unlike the casing this production tubing is not cemented in place (it is usually anchored in place just above the production zone by gripping elements that are latched to the casing's inside wall and by special rubber seals) and hence a joint or a section failure is easily repaired. In addition, it is easy to incorporate various flow control devices and automatic shut off safety valves in the tubing and the casing remains protected from corrosion and erosion caused by hydrocarbons, water and dispersed solids drawn from a well. A well is completed with the installation of the above ground wellhead.

This complex assembly stack of valves, spools, pressure gauges and chokes is commonly called a Christmas tree, a tell-tale sign of the presence of an oil well in an otherwise undisturbed terrain: it was introduced in 1922 and it is connected to the top of a completed well in order to control the flow of oil (see figure 20). A small-diameter gathering pipeline leads from a well to a stock tank and the entire area used for exploratory drilling can be returned to its previous use.

New wells are commonly under enough pressure (due to accumulated gases, water or gravity drainage) to push the oil from the reservoir into the well bore and then all the way to the surface (i.e. the reservoir pressure is higher than the pressure inside the well bore). In reservoirs where pressure is higher than the bubble point pressure the undersaturated oil will contain variable volumes of solution gas, with typical formation volume factor (ratios of reservoir/stock tank barrels) between 1.2–1.6. Oil volume thus shrinks as it reaches the surface but the expanding gas helps a well to flow naturally. Best natural flows come with the presence of cap gas when up to half of the oil in place (but more typically 25–35%) can reach the surface unaided. Natural waterdrive, with underground water displacing oil, is less efficacious, with free-flowing recovery rates of as little as 10% and, rarely, up to 40%. As the extraction proceeds the reservoir pressure declines (sometimes rapidly, in a matter of months, but usually only after many years) and it is necessary to deploy artificial lift. Although some reservoirs, especially those containing heavy oil, do not have sufficient initial pressure and oil production requires pumping from the very beginning.

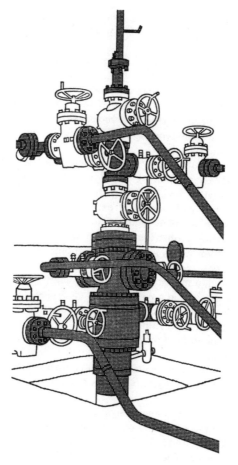

Figure 20 A 'Christmas tree' well-head assembly (courtesy of BP).

Production under natural pressure or aided by a pump lift is classed as primary oil recovery and in most reservoirs it is able to extract only a small share of the oil that was originally present in the formation. The early producers followed an entirely

LIFTING OIL

External energy is needed to lift the fluid in a well bore. This has been done using rod pumps, electrical submersible pumps and also by gas lift. Rod (beam) pumps are readily recognizable because of their characteristic massive assembly – a walking beam that is moved by a pitman attached to a crank and counter weight usually powered by a diesel engine – and because of their ponderous nodding motion.

An electrical submersible pump was used for the first time in Baku in 1917 but the practice spread only after Phillips Petroleum introduced better designs during the 1920s. The latest designs include pumps with longer strokes and slower speeds that result in more complete pump filling and in higher pumping efficiency; a low-profile unit that can work under center-pivot irrigation pipes in cropfields; and an entirely new design that replaces rods with computer-controlled cables. Modern submersibles are multistage centrifugal pumps that are installed just below the fluid in a well bore and electrified via an armored cable. Subsurface hydraulic pumps use power fluid that flows down an inner tubing string; the return flow of this fluid, mixed with the produced oil, goes through the annulus between the tubing strings.

Where gas is readily available it can be used to lower the mass of the liquid column (gas lift systems appeared for the first time during the 1930s).

Artificial lift now dominates oil extraction. In 2005 Iran and Kuwait were the only major oil producers where virtually all wells flowed naturally. And in 2006, only about 6% of the nearly 810,000 operating wells around the world were flowing.

primitive sequence of oil extraction: initially they were producing as much oil as a reservoir's natural pressure allowed (and all too often drilling too many wells to do so), once the natural flow ceased they deployed pumps and once the pumping became uneconomical they considered a reservoir depleted and moved on. Natural gas associated with oil was simply released into the atmosphere or it was flared.

Reservoir engineering, now a key pillar of profitable oil extraction, began to evolve slowly during the 1920s and it progressed more rapidly during the 1930s and 1940s. It has been revolutionized by the deployment of directional and horizontal drilling, by multilateral wells and by new methods of secondary recovery and enhanced production

As already explained (in chapter 3), horizontal drilling diffused rapidly during the late 1980s and 1990s. In addition to the already noted advantages (above all increased production and recovery rates) there are other appealing attributes of the technique: it has made it possible to complete several wells from a single location, a particularly welcome capability when producing from offshore fields (where a single platform may gather oil from many wells), in land locations that are difficult to access and in situations where a number of smaller reservoirs can be reached from a single wellhead; it reduces the number of wells (or, even more importantly, of offshore platforms) needed to develop the reservoir; and it makes it possible to position wellheads away from environmentally sensitive locations and to develop near-shore reservoirs from land.

Reservoir development through the use of multilateral wells was first advocated in 1949 by Alexander M. Grigoryan. In 1953 in Ishimbaineti field (today's Bashkortostan) Grigoryan used downhole turbodrills (i.e. operating without rotating drill strings) to drill the main 575 m deep wellbore that ended just above the pay zone, and from that point he drilled nine branches reaching into the production zone, one with a maximum horizontal reach of 136 m. The world's first multilateral well cost about one and a half times as much as a vertical equivalent but it resulted in a seventeen-fold increase in production, a return that led to an additional 110 such wells being drilled in the field. But because of the significantly higher costs of multilateral drilling the technique's early successes were not followed by widespread adoption. Commercial diffusion of multilateral drilling has lagged about a decade behind the acceptance of horizontal drilling, with increasing numbers of such completions since 1995. The simplest multilaterals are open hole bores from an open hole mother bore and they are possible only in consolidated formations. A more common arrangement has open laterals running from the cased and cemented main bore.

Multilateral wells drilled using mud motors guided by precision geosteering (sometimes done in a fishbone pattern radiating from the main well bore) make it possible to extend the life of ageing oil fields and to achieve optimal reservoir drainage in new finds. Undulating well bores, following a roller coaster oil-bearing formation are now also possible: one completed recently ranged more than 20 m between the trough and the peak.

Intelligent well systems are yet another innovative technique that has acquired the status of a mainstream solution since the year 2000. The first system with permanent monitoring and the ability to control the subsurface flows was installed in 1997 and by 2005 there were more than 200 such installations. Intelligent well systems are aimed at maximizing output and reserve recovery rates by installing sensors, monitoring equipment and completion components (above all control valves, usually as either hydraulically operated or electronically actuated sliding sleeves) that are remotely controlled from the surface; their constant monitoring makes it possible to control, in real time, the flow of water or gas encroachment in producing wells as well as regulating the fluxes in water or gas injection wells. Data from intelligent well systems is used for increasingly complex dynamic simulations of reservoirs. These simulations can help to optimize the extraction rates and to anticipate the reservoir flows and well performance.

Given the cost of such installations they are best suited for high-cost (that is mostly deepwater) wells, for managing the production from multilateral wells and for boosting productivity in old wells in mature oilfields (by better managing the process of secondary and tertiary oil recovery). Intelligent wells are also used to develop marginal fields and to produce oil from heavy oil deposits. Their growing popularity is attested by the fact that their installation was increasing at a compound annual rate of nearly 30% between 2000 and 2005. The North Sea and the Gulf of Mexico are the two oil provinces with the highest number of intelligent wells. But a rapid growth from a tiny base is not a revealing indicator of eventual diffusion. In most cases intelligent wells are still simply too expensive to justify their installation on the basis of improved recovery.

SECONDARY OIL RECOVERY

The primary purpose of secondary recovery is to restore adequate reservoir pressure and to displace oil toward the well bore. This is most commonly achieved with water flooding. Unintentional flooding has been taking place since the earliest decades of oil extraction but, controlled flooding in water injection wells has been used since the 1920s. However, the effect may be less than expected due to the variable permeability of the injected formation, injected water may also break through into a well causing production and processing complications. Oil brought to the surface must be separated from water and from any impurities as well as from gases. The process reaches its limit once the injected fluid constitutes such a high share of the total produced volume that extraction becomes uneconomical.

In large fields secondary recovery means handling huge volumes of water. Al-Ghawār has been producing with the assistance of peripheral water flooding since the early 1960s and in 2003 the water saturation of extracted oil was 33%. The sea-water that

SECONDARY OIL RECOVERY (*cont.*)

is used in the process is delivered by a pipeline from the Gulf and bottom water is discarded, although further treatment may be required to separate water that has become emulsified in the oil.

Water can also be mixed with polymers to enhance its viscosity and to lower its mobility. Surfactants can be introduced to gather oil and to surround it with a barrier, making it easier for the water to push it to the surface. Steam flooding, consisting either of a continuous injection of hot steam or of a cyclical introduction of steam and water into a reservoir, is common in recovering heavy oil.

Immiscible gas injection is a process replicating the natural gas cap drive and it has been used since the 1920s. More common, and much more efficient, miscible gas injection (used since the 1950s) introduces supercritical compressed CO_2 into the gas cap. Field management now routinely relies on optimally distributed gas-injection wells to enhance reservoir pressure.

Other possible methods of improving oil recovery include microemulsion flooding (very expensive); *in situ* combustion whereby heat and steam created by the burning of bitumen is used to drive oil from a formation (rarely used and risky); and microbial recovery, inoculation with suitable bacteria to produce biosurfactants that act as emulsifiers or wetting agents.

Combined primary and secondary recovery can now extract as much as 40–50% of the oil initially in place, that is 20–30% more than in operations without enhanced recovery.

Completing wells under the sea is obviously much more challenging than equivalent operations on land. Flow control devices can be placed above the water line in shallow waters but deep-water drilling has required the development of new subsea production systems. Completed undersea wells (with Christmas tree exposed to the surrounding water, sheltered in housing or buried in the seabed) are connected to manifolds on the ocean floor and tied with electrical umbilicals and flow lines to shallower waters. The new hardware and techniques needed for these completions (subsea trees, remote robotic installations and repairs) were pioneered in the Gulf of Mexico, where the first submerged wellhead was installed in 16 m of water in 1961.

The 1960s saw nearly seventy subsea completions (with wells connected to fixed platforms in waters up to 190 m deep) as well as the first multiple-zone completions tying a number of wells to a single production facility. Increased drilling activity during the 1970s brought the first subsea tree systems that were installed entirely below the seabed and the first applications of diverless installation and maintenance of deepwater production sites (in four wells in the Ekofisk field in the North Sea in 1971). The North Sea was also the site of the world's first floating production system, set up at the Argyll oil field in 1975, and subsequently many similar arrangements have been used at other oil and gas fields in the region as well as offshore Australia and Brazil. The deepest subsea completion so far was a natural gas well in 2,198 m of water installed by the drill ship Discoverer Spirit in 2002.

Operations in waters deeper than 450 m could not use fixed production platforms and the increasing volumes of offshore extractions have required larger production facilities; by the end of the twentieth century these structures included the most massive mobile artefacts ever built. In the 1970s the world's tallest and heaviest drilling and production platform was Shell's *Cognac* in the Gulf of Mexico: at 308 m it exceeded the height of the Empire State Building. In November 1982, *Statfjord B* platform was towed from a construction dock to the Norwegian sector of the North Sea: its four massive hollow concrete columns and storage tanks at its base made it, at just over 800,000 t, the heaviest object ever moved.

In 1989 Shell's *Bullwinkle*, sited in 406 m of water and weighing about 70,000 t, became the world's tallest pile-supported fixed steel platform. In 1983 the first tension-leg platform (TLP) in the Hutton field in the UK sector of the North Sea was anchored by slender steel tubes to the sea floor 146 m below the surface. By 1999 *Ursa* TLP, a joint project of a group of companies lead by the Shell Exploration & Production Company, was the largest structure of its kind (see figure 21). Its total displacement is about 88,000 t (more than a Nimitz-class nuclear aircraft carrier), it rises 146 m above water level and is anchored with sixteen steel tendons to massive (340 t) piles placed into the seafloor 1,140 m below the surface. SPAR, another innovative design, is also moored with steel lines but its deck is supported by a single large-diameter vertical cylinder.

Figure 21 Ursa oil production platform in the Gulf of Mexico.

More than 800,000 oil wells were in production worldwide in 2006 and with a daily extraction of 73 Mbpd (oil only, without NGL) this prorated to nearly 90 b/well a day – but this is a perfect example of a misleading average, both on the international and intranational level. The already noted highly skewed distribution of oil field sizes (see chapter 2) must also apply to individual wells. In 2006 roughly 63% of the world's operating oil wells (just over half a million) were in the US where the average daily flow per well was just ten barrels. But detailed US statistics show that 30% of wells produced less than a barrel a day, some 77% of all wells produced less than ten barrels a day (mean of 2.3) and that the mean for 85% of all wells was just 3.1/bpd. In contrast, the lowest average national well productivity among the OPEC countries was in Indonesia with about 107 bpd, followed by Venezuela with about 165 barrels per well, while the Saudi daily mean was more than 5,700 b per well and the Iranian rate was more than 3,400 b.

Enormous differences in the productivity of oil fields, in their location and in the nature of their flow (natural vs. assisted lift) result in a wide span of production (lifting) costs, with extremes between the least and most expensive operations ranging for more than an order of magnitude. Naturally, supergiant and giant oilfields in the Persian Gulf region have the lowest lifting costs: some wells produce oil at less than twenty cents a barrel, the Saudi oil minister quoted a nationwide mean of less than $1.50/b in 1999. In 2004 a former secretary general of OPEC wrote that in a highly competitive world the organization could produce and sell oil to satisfy the global demand at $5/b. And in 2005 Morris Adelman (the doyen of international oil economics) calculated the average cost of a Saudi barrel at post-2005 prices at $2.90 – but cautioned that the value was too high as it includes the associated natural gas whose value cannot be separated due to the absence of adequate data. Given these realities it is easy to argue that the cartel has been successful in keeping abundance and inexpensive supply at bay and that it has been collecting an enormous transfer of wealth from the rest of the world.

By far the best data on lifting costs are available for the twenty-nine major US-based oil companies that file their statements with the federal Financial Reporting System and that operate not only in the US and Canada but also extensively in Europe and parts of Africa and to a much lesser degree in the Middle East (where national companies dominate) and in the countries of the former USSR. In 2005 their US direct lifting costs averaged $5.39/b, the lowest rate since the late 1970s! Their foreign costs were also lower than at any time during the preceding two decades; they averaged $6.98/b for production in Canada, $5.71 in the EU, $4.09 in Africa, $4.81 in the Middle East, making a worldwide total of $5.13/b. All of these rates are exclusive of taxes: their inclusion raises the US 2005 mean to $7.34/b and the international average to $6.87/b.

Finally, some representative estimates of the energy cost of oil production. The highest energy return on energy investment (EROEI) came with the discoveries of giant and supergiant Middle Eastern oilfields: easily thousand-fold (or even close to ten thousand-fold) at wellhead (i.e. energy equivalent to less than or 0.005% of hydrocarbons discovered was invested in finding that oil). Production costs from these huge reservoirs (including energies for the secondary recovery) are also a relatively small share of the oil present in the ground. Even in the case of two North Sea oilfields, Auk and Forties, the energy invested in their discovery and development was repaid in oil in less than three months. In rich oilfields the net energy ratio can surpass 0.97 or even 0.995. Energy cost of extraction is thus equal to just 0.5–3% of energy in the produced oil, corresponding to EROEI of 33–200. The typical performance of small oilfields is much less impressive.

HISTORY OF OIL PRODUCTION

The historical progress of oil production can be traced fairly accurately from the earliest decades of the industry. The best estimate puts crude oil production (from seeps, pools and hand-dug wells) at about 300 t in 1850; by 1880 the total surpassed 4 Mt; by 1900 the total was 22.5 Mt (half of it from Russia, and 95% of that from Baku, and 9.5 Mt from the US). Between 1900 and 1920 extraction nearly quadrupled to almost 100 Mt and then it doubled in just a decade to 196 Mt in 1936 and on the eve of WWII it rose to 272 Mt. Another doubling took place by 1950 and yet another during the 1950s (to 1.052 Gt in 1960), followed by a 2.2-fold increase during the 1960s to 2.35 Gt in 1970. The peak was reached at 2.87 Gt in 1974; then the production experienced a one-year decline only to reach a new record high of 3.23 Gt in 1979. OPEC's second oil price increase finally made the markets work: by 1983 production fell to 2.76 Gt (a 15% decline) and it did not surpass the

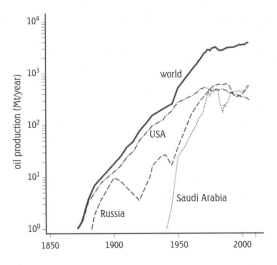

Figure 22 Global oil production, 1859–2007.

HISTORY OF OIL PRODUCTION (*cont.*)

1979 peak until 1994. By the century's end it stood at 3.61 Gt and in 2005 it was close to 4(3.895) Gt (see figure 22).

There have been also some notable shifts, deletions and new appearances on the list of leading producers. In 1950 the US was by far the largest producer and the USSR was a distant second. Fifteen years later the US was still in the lead, followed by the USSR, Venezuela and Kuwait, which was slightly ahead of Saudi Arabia. Norway did not produce a single barrel and China was extracting just over 200,000 bpd. The US lost its primacy to the USSR in 1975 and fell to third place behind Saudi Arabia in 1977. Saudi production peaked in 1980 (at about 85% of the Soviet level) but within five years it declined by two-thirds and the USSR remained the world's largest oil producer until its dissolution in 1991. As the extraction in the USSR's successor states fell, Saudi Arabia became the world's largest producer in 1992, and has held that place ever since.

In 2005 Saudi extraction reached a new record of 11.1 Mbpd, followed by Russia's 9.5, the US remained third (8.2), followed by Iran (4.2), Mexico (3.8) and China (3.8). Canada (3.1), Norway (3.0), UAE (2.8) and Venezuela (2.8) made up the remainder of the top producers. The US is still the country with the highest cumulative extraction: between 1859 and 2005 it produced about 192 Gb of crude oil. The fields that contributed most to this total are the two supergiants, East Texas (flowing since 1931) and Prudhoe Bay in Alaska (producing since 1977), and two California giants, Wilmington (producing since 1932) and Midway-Sunset (since 1901). Russia has the second highest cumulative production, with close to 140 Gb of crude oil by 2005 and Saudi Arabia was third with about 110 Gb. Oil's extraordinarily massive production lends itself to many trivial but revealing calculations and I will cite just three of them. In 2005 the global crude oil extraction (including NGL) amounted to more than 80 Mbpd, almost enough to satisfy the annual oil demand of Finland. In 2005 the world's largest producer, Saudi Arabia, produced more oil in one month than the entire world did in 1900. And in 2005 al-Ghawār's output came very close to matching Japan's annual consumption of liquid fuels.

The best estimates of the nationwide US means show that the EROEI for oil discovery and extraction averaged at least 100 during the 1930s, was about twenty-five in the early 1970s and it has recently been close to twenty. These findings allow two important generalizations. First, there is no doubt that outside of the Middle East the oil industry has been experiencing a secular decline of its EROEI. However, even the latest, and historically low rates compare favorably with the energy cost of coal whose EROEI, particularly after accounting for all transportation, processing and environmental protection costs, is of the same order of magnitude.

Oil transport

The primitive beginnings of oil transport on land included very expensive deliveries by horse-drawn wagons carrying wooden barrels and short leaky wooden pipelines (the first one was built in Pennsylvania in 1865). In 1878 the first major cast-iron pipeline (15 cm in diameter) linked Bradford and Williamsport in Pennsylvania and a year later it was extended to Bayonne in New Jersey (hence known as the Tidewater line). Expansion of pipelines coincided with the introduction of inexpensive steel, made first by the Bessemer process and later by open hearth furnaces. Steel, with its high tensile strength, is superior to cast iron and a fundamental innovation that opened the way for an eventual large-scale expansion of pipeline transport was the invention of the pierce rolling process for the production of seamless steel pipes by Reinhard and Max Mannesmann at their father's file factory in Remscheid in 1885. A few years later they introduced the pilger rolling process that reduces the diameter and wall thickness of pipes while increasing the tube length. The universally used combination of these two techniques is known as the Mannesmann process.

Perhaps the most important non-technical development in the early history of pipelines was their first government regulation, the Hepburn Act passed by Congress in 1906: by making all interstate pipelines common carriers it guaranteed service to all customers at equal cost. Between the two world wars the US remained the only major economy with an increasingly dense pipeline network. During the 1930s came the first lines carrying refined products and these were greatly extended during WWII as new large-diameter lines carried crude and products from Texas and Oklahoma to the largest consuming nodes in the Northeast.

About two-thirds of all US liquid fuel shipments are now carried by pipelines and because of the transport of refined products the total volume carried is more than twice as large as the total crude oil consumption. The Texas-Louisiana coast, Cushing in Oklahoma, Chicago, New York and Los Angeles are the nation's key hubs for oil and product shipments. The country has nearly 90,000 km of oil trunk (mostly 20–60 cm) lines and perhaps as many as 65,000 km of gathering (5–12.5 cm) lines, mainly in Texas, Oklahoma and Louisiana. The most notable US pipeline is the Trans Alaska Pipeline System (TAPS) built between 1975 and 1977 to carry oil (capacity of 1.2 Mbpd) from the supergiant Prudhoe Bay field to the ice-free port of Valdez on Alaska's southern coast. Although it broke no length or diameter records (1,280 km, 120 cm) virtually the entire route crosses permafrost territory and the pipe had to be built on elevated supports above ground and heated to 60°C.

Russia's record of pipeline construction is as old and as notable as the US achievements. The first Russian pipeline from the Baku fields to Nobel's refinery was completed in 1878 and in 1896 Russians began to build one of the first long-distance product pipelines to carry kerosene from Baku (on the Caspian Sea) to Batumi on the Black Sea; the 835 km line was completed in 1906. But a large scale expansion of major trunk lines came only after WWII as an inevitable consequence of the country's enormous territory and of the concentration of its new oil discoveries far from the main centers of consumption in the European part of the country: by 1950 the country had about 5,400 km of oil pipelines, by the time of the USSR's demise their length reached 94,000 km. Because the territory of the former USSR was more than twice as large as that of the US, the US had retained its primacy as the country with the world's densest network of pipelines but the USSR surpassed it in terms of the longest large-diameter lines.

Construction of the 3,662 km long Trans-Siberian line from Tuymazy to Irkutsk began in 1957 (completed in 1964) and in 1959 it was decided to build a branching Druzhba trunk pipeline to supply East Germany (via Poland) through the northern spur, and Hungary and Czechoslovakia through the southern branch, with a total length of more than 6,000 km and mostly with pipe diameter of 102 cm. Later additions extended its overall length to about 8,000 km. In 1973 construction began on the Ust'-Balik-Kurgan-Almetievsk line, 2120 km long and with a diameter of up to 122 cm, to carry up to 90 Mt of crude oil annually from the supergiant Western Siberian Samotlor oilfield to European Russia where it connects to the older lines that now take Western Siberian oil all the way to Central and Western European markets.

Europe's rapid post-1960 conversion from coal to imported crude oil led to the construction of many new pipelines and after major oil discoveries in the North Sea new undersea lines brought fuel to UK, Norway and Denmark. Rising exports led to large-scale pipelined projects in a number of major producing countries, above all in Saudi Arabia and in Iran, and new discoveries of giant oilfields required the construction of the first long-distance pipelines in China. There is no shortage of bold pipeline plans, including what would be the world's

ADVANTAGES OF PIPELINE TRANSPORT

Preference for pipelines as principal long-distance carriers of oil is above all a matter of logistics and cost. Replacing a 1,000-km pipeline carrying 20,000 t of oil a day by tanker trucks (assuming each truck holds 25 t and covers 1,000 km a day) would need a fleet of 1,600 vehicles with a load arriving every 54 seconds. No land transport can be cheaper and only large-scale water-borne transport, that is large river barges and ocean tankers, can move oil less expensively. But pipelines operate with unmatched reliability and safety and hence with minimal environmental impact. They are also quite compact (1 m-diameter pipeline can carry 50 Mt of crude oil a year) and are made from a relatively inexpensive material (steel). Common outside diameters range from 60–140 cm, and pipe sections are usually 18–22 m long.

Oil is pushed through pipelines by centrifugal pumps powered by electric motors, diesel engines or gas turbines that are located at the origin of a line and then at intervals of 30 to 160 km (depending on the terrain crossed by the line and its throughput). Typical oil speed is 5–12 km/hour (hence it may take up to three weeks for Texas oil from Houston to reach New York) and pipelines normally operate non-stop throughout the year, with sections shut down briefly for scheduled maintenance. Crude oil, different refined products or their different grades (especially those of gasoline) are moved through pipelines according to advance schedules. When two very different batches (such as gasoline and diesel) mix at a transport interface they must be reprocessed on arrival. Batches can also be separated by pigs, polyurethane plugs pushed by the transported liquid. Other pigs (with abrasive coatings) are used to strip deposits from the interior of pipes and smart pigs, introduced during the 1960s, storing data on onboard computers or relaying it by telemetry, are used to inspect the integrity of pipes and detect any leakages.

The low operating cost of oil pipelines is illustrated by the following US comparison: they move nearly 20% of all freight

ADVANTAGES OF PIPELINE TRANSPORT (*cont.*)

tonnage but do so with only 2% of the total shipping cost. Energy cost of oil transportation is also relatively low, both in absolute terms and (even more so) when compared to the aggregate energy that they deliver during the course of their long operational life. Steel, the dominant material in pipeline construction, is produced with an equivalent of about 85 t of oil per kilometer for a 60 cm diameter pipeline whose construction requires an equivalent of about 35 t of oil per kilometer for a total cost of about 120 t of oil equivalent, or less than 0.1% of the energy in the oil that the pipeline will carry during (at least) four decades of service.

most expensive oil line between eastern Siberia and the Pacific (Taishet-Nakhodka, nearly 4,150 km long) to bring Siberian oil to Japan.

Early waterborne oil transport was as primitive as the first land transfers: *Elizabeth Watts* was the first brig to take such a shipment (about 200 t of oil stored onboard in kegs) from Philadelphia to London in 1861. Ships with small (and often leaky) built-in iron tanks followed during the 1860s and 1870s, but the first true tanker (carrying oil against the hull) was the English-built 300-t *Glückauf* launched in 1884. Subsequent growth of both typical crude oil tanker capacities and ship sizes was slow. The limited size of the pre-WWI oil market (ships and trains were coal-fuelled, automobile ownership had begun to expand only in the US, and there was no commercial flying) did not require large oil tankers.

The largest vessels reached more than 20,000 dead weight tons (dwt, the weight of cargo plus ship's stores, bunkers and fuel) by 1921 and during the 1920s came better interior framing to make tankers lighter yet sturdier and better pumps and pipes but the typical sizes remained small: during the late 1930s

WORLD'S LARGEST TANKERS

In 1959 *Universe Apollo* was the first 100,000 dwt ship, in 1966 Ishikawajima-Harima Heavy Industries launched the150,000 dwt *Tokyo Maru* and later in the same year the 210,000 dwt *Idemitsu Maru*. By 1973 there were more than 350 very large or ultra large crude oil carriers (with capacities in excess of 300,000 dwt), and ships of 1 million dwt were expected to arrive soon. They were never launched as tanker sizes peaked with the order of Seawise Giant in 1975 and its enlargement three years later. The world's largest ship was hit in 1988 during the Iran-Iraq war but it was subsequently repaired and the 564,763 dwt (nearly 459 m long) vessel was relaunched, renamed twice and now, as *Knock Nevis*, it is moored at Qatar's al-Shahīn oilfield where it serves as a floating storage and offloading unit.

Figure 23 *Iwatesan*, a 300,000 dwt double-hulled VLCC built by Mitsui Engineering & Shipbuilding in 2003.

WORLD'S LARGEST TANKERS (*cont.*)

Supertankers stopped growing not because of insurmountable technical problems or because of excessive cost (economies of scale decline rapidly with size but they still continue) but rather because of operational considerations (see figure 23). Very large crude carriers (VLCC, between 240,00–350,000 dwt) and ultra large crude carriers (ULCC, 350,000–500,000 dwt) can dock only at a limited number of deepwater ports or must offload their cargo at special offshore terminals connected to onshore storage sites and refineries by pipelines (and before these were in place they had to offload their cargo to smaller vessels). A limited number of ports of call makes the use of ultra large tankers less flexible and because of their deep draft supertankers must also follow restricted routes in near-shore waters or channels and they require very long distances while maneuvering and stopping. For example, a typical 250,000 dwt tanker (more than 350 m long, 60 m wide, with a draft of 25 m and average speed of about 12 knots) takes over 3 km (or fourteen minutes) to come to a full stop and its turning diameter is 1.8 km.

tankers rarely carried more than 10,000 dwt. Rapid growth of tanker capacities began only after WWII when the mass produced T-2 tankers (16,000 dwt) were not needed by the military after the conflict's end and when some of the even more numerous Liberty class ships (also 16,000 dwt) were converted to tankers. Rapidly rising post-WWII demand for crude oil in Europe and Japan then stimulated the development of larger tankers and record sizes began to double in less than ten years. As a result, the supertanker designation shifted from 50,000 dwt ships (before the mid-1950s) to 100,000 and then to 200,000 dwt vessels.

Suezmax ships (up to 180,000 dwt) can pass through the canal and shorten the trip from the Middle East to Europe, particularly when they are loaded at Yanbu, on the Saudi Red Sea coast. But the additional distance around Africa, or the long transport routes between the Persian Gulf and Japan, South Korea and China, make little difference to the overall cost of tanker shipping. The vessels are propelled by cheap diesel fuel, incremental costs are thus quite negligible and oil transport by supertankers adds only about half a cent to the retail cost of a liter of gasoline. Some tankers are equipped with steam heating coils in their cargo compartments in order to keep very heavy or highly waxy crude oils or heavy refined products above their pour point.

The energy costs of tanker shipping are equally marginal. Moving Alaskan oil 3,800 km by tanker from Valdez to Long Beach in California requires energy equivalent to only about 0.5% of the transported fuel. And a 300,000 dwt supertanker needs an equivalent of only about 1% of the fuel it carries in order to travel more than 15,000 km from Rās Tanūra, the world's largest loading oil terminal on the Saudi coast of the Persian Gulf (annual capacity 6 Mbpd), to the US East Coast. With rising US oil imports this run has become more common but because the country imports a large share of its needs from Canada, Mexico and Venezuela (nearly 40% of US imports come from the Western hemisphere) and Africa (almost 20%) the Persian Gulf-US East Coast run still moves less oil (not even 20% of US imports) than the already noted Persian Gulf-Europe (via Suez or around the Cape of Good Hope, a trip of forty days) or Persian Gulf-East Asia routes.

The latter route leads through the world's two most notorious shipping chokepoints, the Strait of Hormuz between Iran and Oman and the Strait of Malacca between Indonesia and Singapore. Some 17 Mbpd now pass through the Hormuz (or more than a third of global oil exports) a shipping channel that is just over 3 km wide at its narrowest point. Most of the oil for the world's second (Japan), the third (China) and the fifth (South Korea) largest importers passes through the Strait of Malacca (about 12 Mbpd now and more in the future as China's imports will rise) whose narrowest passage, the Phillips Channel in the Strait of Singapore, is less than 2.5 km wide. Other notable chokepoints with high potential for collisions, sabotage or terrorist attacks are: the Turkish Straits (Bosporus and Dardanelles) that has to be passed by all tankers taking oil from the Black Sea to the Mediterranean; Bab al-Mandab between Djibouti and Yemen, linking the Arab Sea and the Red Sea; Kattegat and Skagerrak between Denmark and Sweden (to move from the Baltic to the Atlantic); and, of course, the Suez and Panama Canals (nearly 4 Mbpd go through Suez, but only about 0.5 Mbpd through Panama).

Finally, a few comparisons to show the global oil (and refined products) trade that was made possible by tankers and pipelines in several revealing perspectives. Global fuel exports were worth almost exactly $1.4 trillion in 2005, or less than 8% of the world's total merchandise trade. In 2005, nearly half (47% or 37.9 Mbpd) of the total crude oil production was sold abroad and exports of refined products amounted to about 12 Mbpd. These transactions were valued at about $780 billion, or roughly 55% of all international fuel sales and their total was higher than the world's importers paid for food (about $680 billion) but lower than the value of automotive products (about $910 billion). Although some forty-five countries export crude oil and more than 140 import it (or buy refined products), the oil trade has always been highly concentrated, both in terms of sales and purchases.

Exports from Middle Eastern countries dominate the global oil trade: in 2005 the region shipped about 45% of all traded oil. In 2005 the world's six largest exporters (with all totals in Mbpd) were Saudi Arabia (9.1), Russia (6.7), Norway (2.7), Iran (2.6), UAE (2.4) and Nigeria (2.3) and they sold just over half of the traded total, while the six largest importers – USA (13.5), Japan (5.2), China (3.4), Germany (2.5), South Korea (2.3) and France (2.0) – bought about 55% of all shipments. The US alone bought about 27% of all traded oil, almost exactly as much as did the whole of Europe. The US was also the largest importer of refined oil products (nearly 30% of the world total), followed by Japan with just over 20%. Altogether the US imported 60% of its liquid fuels in 2006, with Canada being its largest supplier and the Persian Gulf countries providing just over 10% of the US demand. For some time crude oil has also been the single most massively traded commodity; in 2005 shipments of iron ore totaled about 720 Mt, those of natural gas and coal were each roughly 500 Mt – but crude oil sales (1.9 Gt) and refined products (600 Mt) added up to 2.5 Gt of liquid fuels.

Crude oil refining and its products

Crude oil can be burned unrefined and about 0.5% of the global output is still used raw to generate electricity in a few oil-producing countries. Refining, a paragon of value-adding treatment, involves four basic categories of physical and chemical processes. Distillation (fractionation) separates individual cuts (fractions, that is fuels with more homogeneous composition), by heating crude oils first in atmospheric and then in vacuum distillation towers. The yield of light distillates is increased by isomerization, catalytic reforming, alkylation and polymerization. Heavy distillates are subjected to thermal and catalytic cracking. And a variety of processes are used to remove unwanted trace compounds and to prepare environmentally more acceptable final products that are shipped to specific markets. I will explain the essentials of all of these operations through a combination of a brief historic review of advances in refining and a description of a typical process sequence in a large modern refinery.

All early refineries relied on simple thermal distillation, using heat delivered as high-pressure steam in order to separate crude oils into their principal fractions. Consequently, if a particular crude oil contained only a small share of light fractions its thermal refining produced largely medium and heavy liquids. This mattered little until the 1890s when most of the final demand for refined products consisted of kerosene and lubricating oils, but it was a highly unsatisfactory outcome once growing car ownership led to a rapidly increasing demand for gasoline and soon afterwards for diesel oil. Unfortunately, as already explained, most crude oils are not rich in light fractions. Straight thermal distillation of the medium and heavy oils that dominate the global market would yield only 10–15% of the charged volume as the lightest fraction, and the worldwide extent of driving and flying would be restricted by crude oil quality. The industry needed a process that would break C-C bonds to produce lighter compounds and catalytic cracking provided the solution.

Modern refinery consists of a number of complex (sequential and feedback) operations arranged and optimized to convert crude oils into the most valuable combination of specific products (see figure 24). The process starts with desalting that removes not only inorganic salts (whose presence would corrode the refinery pipes, units and heat exchangers) but also suspended solids and water-soluble trace metals. Desalted and dewatered crude oil is heated and led to an atmospheric crude distillation unit (CDU) in whose tower the products are separated by different boiling points into principal cuts that include, gases, straight-run gasoline, light and heavy naphtha, kerosene and atmospheric gas oil. Petroleum gases (light ends) include small alkanes (methane to butane) with boiling points below 0°C. The two lightest gases – methane (CH_4, with

CATALYTIC CRACKING

The first breakthrough in producing lighter products from heavier feedstocks came in 1913 when William M. Burton patented thermal cracking of crude oil. Burton's process relied on the combination of heat and high pressure to break heavier hydrocarbons into lighter fractions. A year later Almer M. McAfee patented the first catalytic cracking process that became commercially available by 1923: crude oil was heated in the presence of aluminum chloride, a compound able to break long-chained hydrocarbon molecules into shorter, more volatile compounds, and gasoline yield was as much as 15% higher compared to thermal cracking. But because the relatively expensive catalyst could not be recovered and reused, thermal cracking (less effective but simpler and cheaper) remained dominant until 1936 when Sun Oil's Pennsylvania refinery in Marcus Hook installed the first catalytic cracking unit designed by Eugène Houdry to produce high-octane gasoline.

Houdry's fixed-bed process allowed for the recovery of the catalyst but it required a temporary shutdown of the refining operation while the aluminosilicate catalytic compound was regenerated. Soon afterwards Warren K. Lewis and Edwin R. Gililand replaced Houdry's fixed catalyst with a more efficient moving-bed arrangement whereby the catalyst circulated between the reaction and the regeneration vessels. This process boosted gasoline yields by 15% and by 1942 90% of all aviation fuel produced for the US war effort was made using this system. An even higher yield was achieved with the invention of powdered catalyst suspended in the air stream (and behaving like a fluid) by four Standard Oil chemists in 1940.

Fluid catalytic cracking (FCC) takes place in a reactor under high temperature (540°C) in less than four seconds. The process of FCC was further improved, beginning in 1960, with the addition of synthetic zeolites. Zeolites are crystalline aluminosilicates whose uniformly porous structure provides an exceptionally active and stable catalyst, improving the gasoline yield by as much as 15%.

CATALYTIC CRACKING (*cont.*)

The last important addition to the techniques of oil refining came during the 1950s when the Union Oil Company developed the process of hydrocracking (proprietary name, Unicracking). This process combines catalysis at temperatures above 350°C with hydrogenation at relatively high pressures, typically at 10–17 MPa. Large-pore zeolites loaded with a heavy metal (platinum, tungsten or nickel) are used as dual function (cracking and hydrogenation) catalysts, the main advantage of the process is that high yields of gasoline are accompanied by low yields of the two lightest, and least desirable, alkanes (methane and ethane).

boiling point at -161°C) and ethane (C_2H_6) – are sent into pipelines or burned to produce energy for refinery operations; processing separates LPG (liquefied petroleum gases, mostly propane and butane) that is used as chemical feedstocks or sold for use as household and industrial fuel for space and process heating and cooking.

Light (straight-run) naphtha (compounds with 5–7 carbons) boil away at 27–93°C and heavy naphtha (6–10 carbons) at 93–177°C. Kerosene is a mixture of alkanes and aromatics with 10–14 carbons and it separates at between 175–325°C. Light gas oil (diesel oil), with alkanes containing 14–18 carbons, boils at between 204–343°C, and is the heaviest cut from a CDU; besides being the second most important road transport fuel it is also used as heating oil and a chemical feedstock. Streams coming from a CDU are first sent to a hydrotreater where they are heated to the maximum of 430°C, mixed with hydrogen and passed over cobalt or molybdenum catalysts: hydrogen's catalytic reaction removes most of the sulfur and nitrogen present in the liquid as hydrogen sulfide and ammonia.

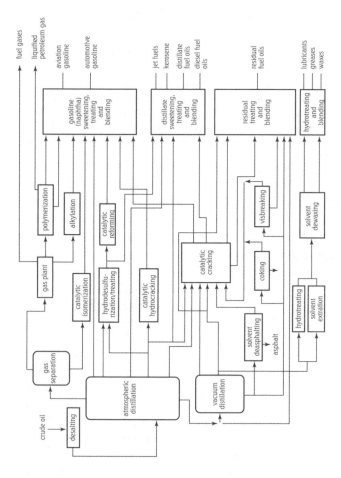

Figure 24 Flow of products in a modern refinery (simplified).

Desulfurized heavy naphtha is then sent to a catalytic reformer to produce a high-octane mixture that, after aromatic extraction and blending, forms the bulk of gasolines. Straight-chained paraffins with low boiling points are converted into branched compounds through catalytic isomerization. Naphtha's content of branched-chained hydrocarbons, as well as the share of aromatics, is also increased by the reforming of naphthenes, a catalytic dehydrogenation and isomerization. Gas oil from the CDU is converted into lighter fractions in a fluid catalytic cracker. Roughly one-third of distillates coming from the CDU are fed to the vacuum distillation unit (VDU) whose reduced pressure facilitates the separation of heavier fractions by decreasing their boiling point.

Vacuum (heavy) gas oil, with a boiling range between 315–565°C is mostly made up of long-chained alkanes (16–40 carbons), cycloalkanes and aromatics. Gas oil from both the CDU and the VDU is transformed into lighter fractions (primarily high-octane gasoline and diesel oil) either in a fluid catalytic cracker or in a hydrocracker. At (figuratively speaking) the bottom of the refinery barrel a viscosity breaker reduces the viscosity of the remaining heavier fractions, coking (extreme thermal cracking with temperatures in excess of 500°C) is used to produce more feed for hydrocracking, lubricants are sent for further processing and heavy fuel oil (largely multi-ringed compounds with boiling points above 600°C) is blown with hot air to produce asphalt.

The various processes used to reform the composition of crude oils – hydrotreating, reforming, isomerization, alkylation, cracking, hydrocracking – have given the refiners flexibility to adjust (within economical limits) the shares of final products. While a typical breakdown of atmospheric distillates from a good quality (light) crude oil would be less than 30% light and heavy naphtha, about 10% kerosene, 15% gas oil and 45% residue, modern refineries can reduce the residue to just 20%

and boost the share of gasolines to 45%. These adjustments make it possible to meet specific national and regional demand. For example while in 2005 the global shares of light and middle distillate and fuel oil were, respectively, 31%, 46% and 11%, the US shares were 46%, 30% and 4%, EU cuts were 23%, 46% and 11% and the Chinese breakdown was 35%, 34% and 13%.

The US, with its high level of road traffic, now consumes almost half of its refined products as motor gasoline and about a quarter as gas and diesel oil; in contrast, Japan's share of gasoline is only 22% but gas and diesel oils account for nearly 30%, and China's respective shares in 2005 were about 17% and 33%. Important shifts, reflecting changing demands, also take place over time. Since 1945 gasoline has accounted for roughly the same share of the US refinery output (about 45%) but the percentage of fuel oil fell from about 20% to less than 5%, while that of kerosene rose from less than 1% to nearly 10%. A closer look at the most important refinery products makes clear their unique qualities and specific uses.

With annual output of about 900 Mt gasolines are the world's most important refined products in terms of price; in mass (or volume) terms gas and diesel oils are more important in the EU, Japan and China but not in the US and Canada. Straight-run naphtha, reformed naphtha and streams from hydrocracking, fluid catalytic cracking, isomerization and alkylation go into their blending. Typical gasoline contains roughly 15% straight-chain alkanes (C_4-C_8), 25% branched alkanes (C_5-C_{10}) and the same share of alkyl benzenes (C_6-C_9). All gasolines are highly volatile and flammable and new environmental regulations require a very low presence (maximum 50 ppm) of sulfur. All of them require additives to improve the efficiency of their conversion as well as to prevent oxidation and rust formation. Gasoline was used only very inefficiently in all early internal combustion engines because

ENGINE KNOCK

In internal combustion engines the compressed fuel-air mixture is ignited from the top of the cylinder by a spark: within half a millisecond an ignition wave starts to propagate downwards, but in the presence of high pressure and high temperature the unignited fuel-air mixture can begin to combust spontaneously, sending a pressure wave in the opposite direction to that of the spreading ignition flame, resulting in a characteristic, and violent, engine knock. Heptanes are particularly prone to this spontaneous ignition caused by compression while octanes are resistant. Retarding the spark reduces the knocking but the only way to avoid it was to operate the engines at low compression ratios and thus lower their efficiency: in early internal combustion engines the ratio was held below 4.3:1 inevitably limiting the engine efficiency and raising worries about the adequacy of post-WWI crude oil supplies. A General Motors team, led by Charles F. Kettering, researched remedial options and identified ethanol as an effective anti-knocking ingredient that made it possible to use gasolines with a higher share of heptanes.

But large-scale production of ethanol was prohibitively expensive and the only other known alternatives (bromine and iodine) were even more costly. This led the company to search for new inexpensive options. A team led by Thomas Midgley first ran some promising trials with tetraethyl tin before confirming, in 1921, that tetraethyl lead was a highly effective anti-knocking agent even when added at concentrations as low as 1/1000 of the fuel's volume. The first leaded gasoline was marketed in February 1923 and its use allowed the compression ratio of internal combustion engines to climb above five and eventually to reach the modern range of 8:1 – 10.5:1. Substantial fuel savings in road transportation were not the only benefit: leaded gasolines made it possible to build more powerful (and hence faster) and more reliable aeroengines.

of a 'knocking' problem that is inherent in Otto's internal combustion engines.

Diesel fuel – blended from fractions obtained by atmospheric distillation as well as from cuts produced by hydrocracking, fluid catalytic cracking, viscosity breaking and coking – is usually the second most important product. The fuel is heavier than gasoline (density of 0.83–0.85 g/mL, compared to 0.73–0.75 g/mL for gasoline) and its lightest category (US No. 1 diesel fuel) is dominated by molecular chains with 9–16 carbons, while the heavier fraction (No. 2) has molecules with 10–20 carbons. Diesel fuel always has 2–3 times more sulfur than the lighter distillates. Due to higher compression ratios diesel engines have higher efficiency than gasoline-fuelled engines (approximately 35% vs. 25%). In addition to passenger cars, trucks, off-road vehicles and ships, diesel fuel is also used to generate electricity during peak demand hours but its sale for domestic heating has declined due to the widespread adoption of natural gas.

Kerosene is the second lightest fraction (C_{11}-C_{13}) of crude oil distillation. Much like gasoline, it is a colorless and a highly flammable liquid that separates from crude oil at 150–275°C. Although still commonly used for lighting and cooking in many modernizing countries (India is a big consumer) and for seasonal heating both in the US and Europe (mainly in portable kerosene heaters), its most important use is to power jet engines (gas turbines) mounted on wings or bodies of both commercial and military aircraft. Kerosene is a better aviation fuel than gasoline because its slightly higher specific density (0.81 vs. 0.71 g/L) results in an energy density that is about 13% higher than that of gasoline (35.1 vs. 31.0 MJ/L), an important consideration when the volume of fuel stored in aeroplane wings and fuselages is obviously limited.

Moreover, the slightly heavier fuel is also cheaper than gasoline and because it is less volatile it has lower evaporation losses at high altitudes and a lower risk of fire during refuelling and ground storage, an attribute that also results in less flagrant, and hence more survivable, crash fires.

Fuel oil is a collective label for a large category of distillate and residual liquids with widely differing properties and with a confusing taxonomy. They are usually divided into six classes. Fuel oil no. 1 is essentially the straight-run kerosene, no. 2 corresponds (except for the additives) to diesel fuel and it is also used as household heating oil. Light fuel oils, distillate fuel oils and gas oil are their common synonyms. No. 4 oil is the most commonly used kind of fuel in powerful marine diesel engines; it contains up to 15% residual oil and hence it is less volatile than automotive diesel (fuel oil no. 2). Fuel oils used in waterborne transportation are usually called bunker fuels. Worldwide statistics show bunker sales of nearly 4 Mbpd in 2005, with the highest national rates (in the US, Netherlands and Singapore) reflecting the presence of the largest oil processing facilities. The two heaviest fuel oils (no. 5 and 6) are commonly called residual oils or heavy fuel oils. No. 6 used to be the most common choice to replace coal in electricity generation but due to very high sulfur levels it was replaced by natural gas, or even by coal (with desulfurization). But coal-fired electricity generating plants use heavy fuel oil to initiate the combustion in their boilers (much like kindling for woodfires).

What remains at the bottom of the barrel cannot be used as fuel but it has valuable non-fuel applications. Some refining processes yield only negligible shares of lubricants and waxes, and in 2005 the nationwide US means of these two final product categories were, respectively, just 1% and 0.1%. Heavier semi-solids and solids are more abundant: in 2005 just over 5% of crude oil delivered to refineries ended up as petroleum coke and nearly 3% was shipped out as asphalt and road oil. Asphalts are chemically even more complex than residual fuel oils and the unique properties of these thermoplastic (soft when heated, hard when cooled) materials have made them one of the most ubiquitous constituents of our constructed world. Asphalts are either straight-run products or (for higher viscosity) are made by blowing air through hot liquid asphalt. Polymers, including polybutadiene in the form of ground tires, can also be added.

Oil refining is by far the most energy-intensive part of the entire sequence of liquid fuel production. US data shows that, on average, the country's refineries consume an equivalent of about 11% of the energy in the processed crude oil, mostly as hot steam, electricity and gases. After subtracting the non-fuel products (lubricants, tar, asphalt) the net energy content of refined fuels is about 85–88% of the energy in the crude oil. Specific studies indicate that gasoline contains 6–10 times more energy than the energy cost of its refinery.

Crude oil refining, producing a wide variety of highly flammable gases and liquids, requires safety precautions in locating the processing and storage facilities, preventing spills and facilitating fire fighting. Minimum spacing of 60–75 m is mandatory for separation of units within a refinery and typical throughputs of about 2.5 t of crude oil/m^2 means that a large (500,000 bpd) facility requires at least 1,000 hectares, although they can be much larger.

In 2005 the worldwide capacity of 661 operating refineries produced 85 Mbpd. Predictably, the largest consumers of liquid fuels had the largest total refining capacities. The US led with about 17 Mbpd, followed by China (6.5), Russia (5.4) and Japan (4.5). As for the largest oil companies, Exxon Mobil and Royal Dutch Shell could each process more than 5 Mbpd in their refineries located around the world, while the aggregate capacities of BP and China's Sinopec approached 4 Mbpd. Because of the rising demand for refined products this capacity was less than 5% larger than the aggregate consumption of crude oil, and among the major consumers of liquid fuels only Russia had a large capacity surplus while the US, Japan and China were all net importers of refined fuels.

As with so many other industrial processes, the closing decades of the twentieth century have seen a trend towards consolidation and increasing unit sizes (leading to economies of scale) in crude oil refining. For example, in 1980 the US had just over 300 refineries, nearly as many as right after WWII, but by 2000 the total had halved to about 150. Large modern refineries now commonly process in excess of 100,000 barrels per day, that is at least 5 Mt of crude a year, and the top ten produce in excess of 500,000 bpd. The world's largest refinery in 2006 was Venezuela's Cardon/Judibana in Falcon with the capacity of 940,000 bpd. Three of the world's ten largest refineries were in South Korea, including Ulsan, the second largest (817,000 bpd), and three belonged to Exxon Mobil (Jurong Island in Singapore, Baytown in Texas and Baton Rouge in Louisiana). The world's third largest refining complex was in Jamnagar in India, the expanded Saudi Rās Tanūra (550,000 bpd) was the largest refinery in the Middle East and Europe's largest facility was Pernis in the Netherlands.

Refineries usually have on-site capacity for storing enough crude oil for two weeks of operation. Voluminous storage is also needed at export oil terminals to fill the tankers and at the starting points of large pipelines to dispatch the custom batches of crude oil or refined products. Much smaller storage tanks are common at many industrial establishments. By far the largest oil storage is the US Strategic Petroleum Reserve that began to fill in 1977. Crude oil is stored deep underground in four massive salt caverns along the Texas and Louisiana Gulf Coast. The maximum capacity is 727 Mb and the reserves stood at 688 Mb in January 2006. This reserve represents about two months of US oil imports and private company reserves increase this to nearly 120 days, well above the International Energy Agency's requirement of 90 days of import protection.

Aggregate commercial oil stocks in OECD countries have been recently fluctuating between 2.4–2.7 Gb. Consequently, the Western world is now much better prepared to weather any sudden, large-scale oil import interruptions than during the 1970s, and China has followed this example and has recently been filling its new strategic oil reserve.

5

How long will oil last?

This chapter's title is a loaded question with multiple answers. The most obvious answer – if the question is taken literally and purely in terms of physical presence – is as long as the planet Earth. Even the best conceivable enhanced recovery techniques will still leave behind a substantial share of the oil originally present in reservoir rocks. More importantly, the excessive cost of discovering and producing liquid oil that is stored in countless tiny, marginal or virtually inaccessible formations, and unappealing returns on extracting liquid hydrocarbons from most of the known oil sands, oil shales and tar deposits will ensure that a significant share of the oil originally in place in the Earth's crust will be never brought to the surface.

If the question means simply how long there will be some commercial production of crude oil then the answer is also easy: definitely throughout the entire twenty-first century. Even those who argue that the peak of global oil extraction is imminent must concede that we have yet to discover many giant reservoirs, and the historical experience shows that some of these accumulations can remain in commercial production for over a century. And there is a good probability that this answer holds even if the volume of oil to be commercially produced by 2100 were to amount to a still significant share, say 5–10%, of the global energy demand. But I will not try to answer the question of how long crude oil will remain the single most important fossil fuel in the global primary energy supply, nor will I predict when global oil extraction will reach its peak and begin to decline. Answers to these questions are contingent on the unknown magnitudes and trends of many variables and any new predictions of the peak production year would only extend an already long list of failed forecasts of this kind.

What I will do instead is to provide a proper historical perspective on oil's role in the global energy supply. Then I will survey the fallacies and facts concerning the currently fashionable catastrophic prognoses of an imminent end of the oil era – the sentiment embodied in publications whose titles claim that we have already reached the production peak, that the party's over, or, in the most extreme fashion, in Richard C. Duncan's Olduvai theory, that the decline of oil extraction will plunge humanity back to a life comparable to that in the famous gorge where some of the first primitive hominids lived 2.5 million years ago. Finally, I will look beyond oil, outlining briefly some major means of providing liquid fuels from sources other than conventional crude oil.

Oil in the global energy supply

If oil's importance were to be judged by the frequency with which the words oil, crude oil or petroleum are mentioned in the media or by politicians, the inevitable conclusion would be that no other source of energy is more important for the survival of civilization. This would be an incorrect and indefensibly exaggerated notion. Undoubtedly, liquid fuels have had an enormous impact on the modern way, and quality, of life, but outside of North America they became very important only during the last two generations, after 1960 in Europe and Japan, and since the 1980s in the populous countries of Asia. Global dependence on oil is thus a relatively new phenomenon, and this reality should forcefully remind us that we should not exaggerate the fuel's indispensability: we had ingenious industrialized societies capable of delivering a decent quality of life long before oil consumption rose to its current level – and there will be prosperous societies supporting a good quality of life long after liquid hydrocarbons have become minor constituents of the global energy supply.

ENERGY TRANSITIONS

Pre-hydrocarbon industrializing societies were energized by coal and also by the generation of hydroelectricity. Coal, the quintessential fuel of the nineteenth century's industrialization, continued to dominate the global supply of commercial energy during the first half of the twentieth century: its share declined slowly, from about 95% of the industrial total in 1900 to nearly 80% of the total in 1930 and to just over 60% by 1950. Meanwhile, crude oil provided just 4% of the world's primary energy in 1900, 16% by 1930 and 27% by 1950 when natural gas supplied about 10% of the total (see figure 25). In many leading economies coal was much

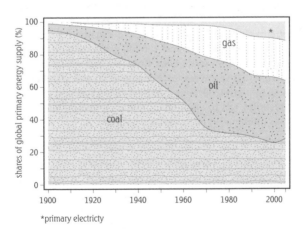

*primary electricty

Figure 25 Global shares of primary energies, 1900–2006.

ENERGY TRANSITIONS (*cont.*)

more dominant: even by 1960 its share in primary energy supply was nearly 60% in Japan, 61% in France, 77% in the UK and 80% in Germany, at that time fuelling the country's impressive economic expansion.

Global transition from coal to hydrocarbons accelerated during the 1960s: 1962 was the first year when coal provided less than half of the world's primary energy. Later, because of oil's numerous advantages, even the two rounds of OPEC's oil price increases could not stimulate coal's comeback. The most important factors that explain coal's continuing retreat are the relatively high cost of its underground extraction, its inflexibility of use and the considerable environmental impact of its production and combustion (the latter including acid precipitation and high carbon emissions).

But there is no doubt that the post-1972 OPEC-driven oil price rises have definitely helped to slow down coal's global retreat, from about 34% of the total supply of primary commercial energy in 1970 to 30% by 1990 and 23% by the year 2000; then, thanks to the surge of coal mining in China and India, came a rebound to 28%. And, coal remains more indispensable than oil even in the US, a society addicted to massive consumption of gasoline and kerosene: slightly over half of America's electricity is now generated by burning coal (the rest coming from nuclear and hydro-generation and from gas-fuelled turbines, with oil contributing a mere 3%). If that coal were to disappear what would then electrify half of all refineries, gasoline pumps at filling stations, street lights or car factories, not to mention incubators for premature babies or machines used during heart by-pass surgery

The best global aggregate count indicates that during the twentieth century coal and crude oil supplied roughly the same amount of primary energy, each approximately an equivalent of 125 Gt of oil, but during the century's second half crude oil's energy surpassed that of coal roughly by a third. Refined oil products became the world's leading source of fossil fuels in

1966 and their share peaked during the 1970s at about 44%; by 1990 it was down to 37%, then it rebounded (thanks to low oil prices) to 41% by the year 2000, but by 2005 crude oil's share slipped to 36% of global primary energy supply, the lowest it has been since the early 1960s. This long-term view puts the importance of crude oil in global energy supply into a proper historical perspective. By 2006 oil had been the largest component of the global primary energy supply for only forty years and during that period its consumption rose more than 2.3 times, from about 1.65 to 3.9 Gt a year (or more than 81 Mbpd).

But crude oil has never reached coal's massive dominance and despite the continued absolute growth of its consumption it has actually been in relative retreat as coal's Asian expansion and greater worldwide reliance on natural gas combined to supply just over half of all commercial energy in 2005. And with the retreat of liquid fuels from electricity generation (less than 7% of all refined fuels were burned in power plants in 2005) and residential uses such as heating and cooking (now also less than 7% of global demand for liquids), the consumption of refined oil products has become even more concentrated in the transportation sector. But because this sector has become such a critical component of all affluent economies and because driving and flying are such ubiquitous activities, it is no exaggeration to conclude that at the beginning of the twenty-first century modern civilization is defined in many important ways by its use of liquid fuels and hence it will go to great lengths to ensure their continued supply.

And it must be repeated that this importance goes beyond the reliance on high-performance fuels, be they for cars or aeroplanes: oil-derived lubricants are indispensable for countless industrial tasks, modern transportation infrastructures are unthinkable without oil-derived paving materials, and syntheses of scores of plastics begin with oil-derived feedstocks. All of these benefits derive from the extraction of a resource that is not renewable on a civilizational timescale, and since the mid-1990s the questions about its durability have been receiving increasingly worrisome answers from some oil geologists whose arguments have been given prominent coverage by the media. Nearly all of those who argue that the peak of global oil production is imminent do not foresee any subsequent comfortable plateau but a rapid decline and assure us that its inevitable consequences will be the end of modern prosperity and an intensifying fight over the dwindling oil resources. I will deconstruct these scares and show why such bleak scenarios are not likely to prevail.

Oil peaks

The basic assumptions tirelessly repeated by the proponents of the theory of an imminent peak of global oil production are as follows. When we compare the total volume of the estimated ultimate recovery (EUR) of oil with the worldwide cumulative production we see that (depending on the somewhat uncertain size of EUR) we have already extracted half of the EUR or are about to do so in a matter of years. At that time global oil production reaches its peak and because its complete cycle must follow a function described by a normal (bell-shaped, Gaussian) curve (with the area beneath the curve equal to EUR), the peak must be followed by a fairly steep decline. Given the importance of oil for modern civilization this inevitable decrease in annual oil production will have enormous consequences, with some of the leading peak oil theorists going as far as writing obituaries of modern civilization.

Ivanhoe believes that an early end of the oil era will bring "the inevitable doomsday" that will be followed by "economic implosion" that will make "many of the world's developed societies look more like today's Russia than the US." For

Richard Duncan the peak is "a turning point in human history" leading to massive unemployment, breadlines, homelessness and a catastrophic end of industrial civilization. In fact, all of the leading proponents of the theory of the imminent peak of global oil extraction (Colin Campbell, Jean Laherrère, L.F. Ivanhoe, Kenneth Deffeyes) resort to alarmist arguments. Their writings and speeches mix incontestable facts and sensible arguments with indefensible assumptions and caricatures of complex processes as they ignore those realities that do not fit their preconceived conclusions.

Their conclusions are based on simplistic interpretations. Values of EUR are not at all certain, and tend to rise with better understanding of petroleum geology, with frontier exploration and with enhanced recovery techniques. Moreover, the proponents of an imminent peak of global oil extraction disregard the role of prices, they ignore historical perspectives, and they presuppose the end of human inventiveness and adaptability. But it is precisely their bias and their catastrophic message that have attracted the mass media (ever eager to spread new bad news) and impressed a scientifically illiterate public. My critique rests on three fundamental realities. First, these recent peak oil worries are only the latest instalment in a long history of failed peak forecasts. Second, the claim of peak-oil advocates that this time the circumstances are really different and hence their forecasts will not fail mixes correct observations with untenable assumptions. Third, and perhaps most importantly, when contemplating a world with little or no oil, a gradual decline of global oil production does not have to translate into any economic and social catastrophes.

Public concerns about running out of fossil fuel resources date to 1865 when William Stanley Jevons, a leading economist of the Victorian era, published a book in which he concluded that it is "of course . . . useless to think of substituting any other kind of fuel for coal" and that the falling coal output must spell the end of Britain's national greatness. In reality, the UK's coal extraction continued to expand until the second decade of the twentieth century and its subsequent decline had nothing to do with the exhaustion of resources, and everything to do with the arrival of new fuels. In 2005 the UK's remaining coal reserves still amounted to hundreds of millions of tons but extracting the fuel was an unappealing proposition compared to producing crude oil and natural gas from the North Sea. In 2005 the world's proved reserves of coal were nearly one Tt, and this total could be multiplied with more exploration and with advanced mining techniques. Clearly, coal's relatively rapid post-1950 retreat has had little to do with 'running out.'

OIL'S REPEATED END

Published reports about the imminent end of oil production can be traced as far back as the 1870s, and fears about running out of liquid oil were quite strong in the US during the early 1920s. But the most influential argument was made by M. King Hubbert who postulated that mineral resource extraction follows an exhaustion curve that has the shape of normal (symmetrical, bell-shaped) distribution: its peak is immediately followed by a decline whose course mirrors the production rise. Hubbert used this approach to accurately predict the peak of US oil extraction in 1970, and the symmetrical exhaustion curve thus acquired the status of an infallible forecasting tool: once the recoverable resources are known and the past production is plotted then a symmetrical continuation of the curve shows the peak extraction year, declining production and the timing of eventual resource exhaustion.

Hubbert's own forecast put the peak of global oil extraction between the years 1993 and 2000: in reality, global output in 2005 was 23% above the 1993 level, a substantial error that is that never cited alongside the correct prediction of the timing (although not of the level) of the US peak. In 1977 the Workshop on Alternative Energy Strategies set the global oil peak as early as 1990 and most

OIL'S REPEATED END (*cont.*)

likely between 1994 and 1997. In 1978 Andrew Flower wrote in *Scientific American* that "the supply of oil will fail to meet increasing demand before the year 2000." In 1979 the CIA believed that the global output must fall within a decade. In 1990 a USGS study put the peak of non-OPEC oil production at just short of 40 Mbpd before 1995 – but the actual output was more than 47 Mbpd in 2005. Some of the latest peak-of-oil proponents have already seen their forecasts fail: Campbell's first peak was to be in 1989, Ivanhoe's peak was in 2000, Deffeys set it first in 2003 and then, with ridiculous accuracy, on Thanksgiving, 2005.

One would think that this record would dissuade more entries, but the true believers cannot resist enlarging this list of failures. Now we are told that missing a year or half a decade is irrelevant and that the failure of forecasts produced during the 1970s or 1980s should not be used to argue for a high probability (or certainty) of future failures. Their principal argument is that, unlike 20–30 years ago, exploratory drilling has already discovered some 95% of the oil that was originally in place in the Earth's crust. Consequently, more frantic and more extensive drilling efforts will make no difference: all it will do is discover the small volume of remaining oil faster. And, they also argue that efficiency improvements (even outlawing SUVs) or a new-found frugality in affluent countries cannot make any fundamental difference: the slower increase in global oil demand (the increase itself being guaranteed by the huge oil needs of modernizing countries) would only slightly postpone the timing of the peak.

Claims about an imminent peak of global oil extraction followed by a precipitous demise of the oil era ignore several fundamental facts. To begin with, there is the most obvious factual correction: even if we were to subscribe to the inevitability of global oil extraction peaking before the year 2010 the Hubbertian reality is that half of all oil is yet to be extracted after that date, and the decline close to a normal curve shape would mean that we would still have more than a century of oil production ahead of us. This means, for example, that a symmetrical curve with the peak at, say, 85 Mbpd in 2010 would imply global extraction of 65 Mbpd in 2030 and nearly 50 Mbpd by 2050. Clearly, the catastrophist belief that the oil era is nearly over is false even when we posit an imminent peak in oil production.

Proponents of an early oil peak are correct in noting an unfortunate absence of rigorous international standards in reporting oil reserves and in pointing out that many officially claimed oil reserve totals (when national figures either do not change at all from year to year or take sudden large jumps) have been politically motivated and should not be trusted. But this uncertainty cuts both ways: if there are politically motivated overestimates of oil reserves there is also a considerable uncertainty about the volume of ultimately recoverable oil. We will know the true extent of oil in place only once we have explored all of the world's sedimentary basins (including deep offshore waters) with an intensity that matches that of the land exploration of North America and the near-shore sector of the Gulf of Mexico. Morris Adelman put it succinctly: "To know ultimate reserves, we must first have ultimate knowledge. Nobody knows this, and nobody should pretend to know."

And yet there is no end of this pretending. Peak oil writings endlessly stress Hubbert's triumph of accurately forecasting the US oil production peak in 1970. But what they ignore is hardly trivial. First, his peak forecast was 20% lower than the actual production peak of 11.3 Mbpd. Second, his peak forecast was based on an EUR of 200 Gb, the total that he himself had raised from the 150 Gb that had he estimated just a few years earlier – but between 1859 and 2005 the US oil industry had already produced 192 Gb, it is still the world's third largest producer of crude oil, and it had 32 Gb of remaining reserves. Clearly, the post-peak decline of US oil production has not been a mirror image of the incline, and the country's oil extraction has not followed a symmetrical curve: in fact, the 2005 extraction was nearly 70% higher than Hubbert's forecast, and the cumulative production between 1970 and 2005 was about 15 Gb larger, or six times the country's 2005 output (see figure 26).

Tellingly, these notable misses are never mentioned by the proponents of an imminent peak of global oil production and Hubbert's forecasting record continues to receive much unmerited and uncritical admiration. I believe that this celebrated peak oil forecasting 'success' should raise some serious doubts not only because of its substantial errors but also because of its general applicability. Hubbert underestimated the US EUR because he had no knowledge of the Prudhoe Bay supergiant or of coming giant finds in the Gulf of Mexico. As the rest of the world has been explored with considerably lower intensity than the US it is obvious that any EUR is just that, an estimate subject to revision, not a fixed total. Indeed, one of the main

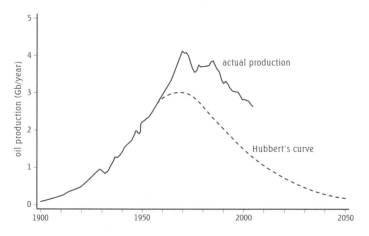

Figure 26 Hubbert's forecast of US peak oil production and the subsequent extraction decline – and the actual 1970–2006 course.

peak oil proponents, Colin Campbell, raised his own EUR from 1.578 Gb in 1989 to 1.95 Gb in 2002, a nearly 25% increase in just a dozen years.

Given all these points I currently see no persuasive reason to choose the most conservative estimates of the ultimately recoverable conventional oil offered by the advocates of an early peak rather than the much higher totals favored by other geologists. Most notably, the latest assessment by the US Geological Survey (and hardly the final total) offers the following division among the three key categories: by the late 1990s roughly 710 Gb of oil were produced worldwide, leaving about 890 Gb of remaining known reserves; nearly 690 Gb should come in the future from reserve additions in currently known fields, and roughly 730 Gb are yet to be discovered, giving an EUR of about 3.020 Tb.

All of these figures are the means of 95%, 50% and 5% probability estimates, but even the first confidence limit (near certainty) puts the undiscovered reserves of conventional oil at 400 Gb, that is nearly three times as much as a typical claim by those who see an imminent peak of global oil extraction. According to the USGS the following six basins have the largest resources of undiscovered conventional oil: the Mesopotamian Foredeep Basin, the West Siberian Basin, the as yet completely unexplored East Greenland Rift Basin, the Zagros Fold Belt, the Niger Delta and the Rub al-Khali Basin of eastern Saudi Arabia. In North America the best prospects for major new oil discoveries are in northern Alaska, in the Canadian Arctic and in the Gulf of Mexico.

In Latin America large reserve additions will come in Venezuela and in Brazil's offshore waters, perhaps most importantly in Foz do Amazonas, in the delta of the river. Most of Africa's untapped oil resources are in waters off Congo and Niger, but significant potential remains in Algeria and Libya. In the Middle East both of the two leading producers, Saudi Arabia and Iran, will see substantial new discoveries, as will Iraq. The latest indicator of this potential is the discovery of a major new Saudi oil and gas field 70 km south-east of al-Ghawār in the Eastern province that was announced in February 2007. Elsewhere in Asia prospects are not that great either in China or in Indonesia but Kazakhstan's huge oil resources remain largely untapped and more oil will be found in the enormous Timan-Pechora Basin west of the Urals. Europe's most promising unexplored regions are the offshore waters of the Atlantic margin west of Scotland.

To sum up, the entire notion of an imminent peak of global oil production is based on three key claims: that recoverable oil resources are known with a high level of confidence; that they are fixed; and that the history of their recovery is subsumed by a symmetrical production curve. None of these claims is true. EUR cannot be known with a high degree of confidence as long as large areas of the Earth remained unexplored or only cursorily assessed, and it is not fixed, as values initially cited for an oilfield's EUR tend to grow with time due to additional drilling and to higher recovery rates. This means that EUR for recently discovered fields definitely underestimate their eventual cumulative production. And the history of US oil extraction is far from being the only case of not following a symmetrical production curve.

The shape of the curve (incline or decline) is also greatly influenced by adjustments in demand, a phenomenon clearly demonstrated by the decline and stagnation of global oil consumption between 1979 and 1994. Even greater discontinuities are possible if deliberate management were to shape the profile of future oil demand. If a looming physical shortage of oil were to become a matter of humanity's survival, then clear priorities could ensure an extended period of adequate supply by allocating the refined fuel according to a firm hierarchy of priority uses. Fuel for agricultural machinery, indispensable aviation and feedstock for essential petrochemical syntheses would be in the first category;

fuels for long-distance transport of perishable goods in the second (but all railway traffic should be electrified); and gasoline and diesel for passenger cars would get the lowest ranking.

Consequently, a large number of future production curves can be drawn on the basis of preferred information (see figure 27). EUR of 1.8 Tb of which only 150 Gb remain to be discovered would mean that world oil extraction is already at its peak, while EUR of about 3 Tb would (depending on the future rates of consumption) imply a peak of conventional oil extraction sometime after 2020 and mean that global production during the 2040s could still be as high as in the early 1980s. But all of these assessments convey an inappropriately narrow resource perspective. As Laherrère (one of the most vocal proponents of an early peak oil production) conceded, with the addition of the median reserve estimates of natural gas liquids (200 Gb; USGS put it at about 325 Gb) and non-conventional oil (700 Gb) there would be still some 1.9 Tb of oil to be produced, double the amount of his estimate for liquid crude oil alone.

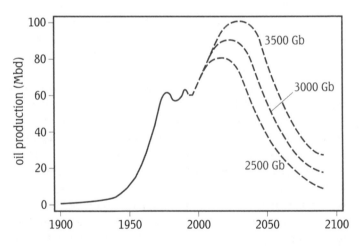

Figure 27 Possible oil production curves during the twenty-first century.

In 2006 an assessment by Cambridge Energy Research Associates took these unconventional resources into account and it put the global oil resource base (including the historical cumulative production if 1.08 Tb) at 4.82 Tb (and likely to grow) which means that 3.74 Tb still remain to be tapped and that what is ahead for the global oil production of the next half a century or so is an undulating plateau rather than any steep decline mirroring the historical run-up. But even if we had a perfect knowledge of the world's ultimately recoverable oil resources the global oil production curve could not be drawn without also knowing the future oil demand. This is impossible because demand will be driven, as in the past, both by predictable forces (including growing populations and higher disposable income) and by unpredictable political and socio-economic changes and, above all, by new technical advances.

To quote Adelman once again: "To predict ultimate reserves, we need an accurate prediction of future science and technology." Of course we do not have this and three prominent historic examples illustrate this ignorance. In 1930 nobody could have predicted the introduction of commercial jet aircraft by 1960, an innovation that created a large new consumer of kerosene. In 1960 nobody could have predicted oil prices rising by an order of magnitude as a result of OPEC's actions, a political shift that, for the first time since the 1860s, led to a notable decline in global oil demand. And in the early 1980s, as oil prices set new records, nobody could have predicted that in 2005 half of the passenger-carrying vehicles in the US would be gasoline-guzzling SUVs, pick-up trucks and vans.

Technical, social and economic shifts can obviously boost or depress future demand and any linear assumptions based on the past rates (be they longer lasting or short-term) are risible. US oil demand rose 50% between 1965 and 1973 but less than 2.5% during the two decades between 1979 and 1999; Chinese consumption jumped nearly 16% in 2004 but less than 3% in

2005. Which one of these values should we use for a truly long-range (say half a century) forecast?

And, quite inexplicably, those who forecast an imminent peak of global oil production and a rapid end of the oil era completely ignore fundamental, and proven, economic realities and assume that future demand is immune to any external factors. This is patently false: an indisputable peak followed by precipitous decline in production would not trigger an unchecked bidding for the remaining oil but would rather accelerate an ongoing shift to other energy sources. OPEC learned this lesson in the early 1980s when record high prices were followed not only by the decline of oil's share in global energy supply but also by an absolute decline in global oil demand and a drastic fall in price (by about 60% for an average OPEC barrel between 1981 and 1986).

As already explained (see chapter 1) that cut in demand was a result of powerful technical adjustments that were triggered by high oil prices – and similarly enormous opportunities for oil savings in road transport remain untapped. All we have to do is to resume the adjustments that were set aside by a generation of post-1984 low oil prices. These realities led Sheikh Ahmed Zaki Yamani, a former Saudi oil minister, to remark that high prices will only hasten the day when OPEC will be left with untouched fuel reserves because new efficient techniques could cut deeply into the demand for automotive fuels and lead to non-oil alternatives, leaving much of the Middle Eastern oil in the ground forever.

The discrepancy between the wishful thinking of imminent peak oil advocates and real world realities is also easily demonstrated by asking the following questions. If we have recently been discovering the very last of all known recoverable resources should not the finding of new oil reservoirs be much more costly than in the past? And if there is an imminent peak of oil extraction should not then the prospective shortage of the precious fuel result in relentlessly rising prices and should not buying a barrel of oil and holding onto it be an unbeatable investment? These conclusions are patently wrong. Oil is not getting either intolerably more expensive to find or to develop, and a barrel of a high-quality crude, say West Texas intermediate, bought at $12.23/b in 1976 as a nest-egg for retirement and sold before the end of 2006 at $60/b would have earned (even when assuming no storage costs) about 1.2% a year, a return vastly inferior to almost any guaranteed investment certificates and truly a miserable gain when compared with virtually any balanced stock market fund (and a 1980 barrel sold in 2005 would have resulted in a nearly 40% loss!).

Finally, regardless of the actual rate of oil extraction and the eventual date of the highest annual production of oil from conventional resources, there is no reason to see the transition to the post-oil era as a period of unmanageable difficulties or outright economic and social catastrophes. Historical evidence is clear: energy transitions have always been among the most important stimuli of technical advances (think of new prime movers, new materials and new energy converters), promoting innovation (such as the profound managerial and organizational changes brought by computers), higher efficiency (for example, a gas turbine vs. steam engine) and resource substitution (like the substitution of coke made from coal for charcoal from disappearing forests during the late eighteenth and nineteenth centuries). Their outcomes – coal replacing wood, oil replacing a great deal of coal, now natural gas already replacing a great deal of oil – have shaped modern industrial, and post-industrial, civilization, leaving deep imprints on the structure and productivity of economies as well as on the organization and the quality of life of affected societies.

To think that these stimuli will cease with a gradual move away from oil is baseless: they have actually been at work for some time, and the effects can be seen in macroeconomic terms as well as in everyday experiences. In 2005 the world's largest economy was only half as oil-intensive as it was in 1973, during the year of OPEC's first large price increases. Remarkably, nearly the same rate of improvement has applied to the global economy. In 1973 the gross world economic product (GWP) was about $21 trillion (in constant 2005 monies) which means that with oil consumption of 2.75 Gt it required roughly 130 kg of crude oil to produce $1,000 of GWP. In 2005, with the GWP at $60 trillion and oil consumption at 4.1 Gt less than 70 kg were needed for every $1,000 of GWP, nearly a 50% reduction!

This impressive decline has been achieved through a combination of the higher efficiencies with which we now convert refined oil products and their substitution by gaseous hydrocarbons, coal and non-fossil energies. Changes in home heating illustrate the effects of all of these factors. In 1975 tens of millions of households that used fuel oil for heating converted it in their oil furnaces with efficiencies that were typically around 50%, recovering no more than half of the fuel's chemical energy as heat inside a house; natural gas is now the dominant heating fuel and even the so called mid-efficiency furnaces have efficiencies of nearly 70% and a high-efficiency furnace in my basement converts 95% of chemical energy into heat. Moreover, many new homes that do not have access to pipelined gas and that would once have been heated by fuel oil are now heated by electricity because their superinsulated construction has lowered their overall energy demand.

But even with remarkable technical advances there is no doubt that energy transitions present enormous problems for the providers of energies that are being replaced (OPEC members certainly do not look forward to any early end of the oil era), that they necessitate scrapping or reorganization of many old infrastructures (think of all the oil tankers, pipelines and refineries), and that they require the introduction of entirely new links, procedures and practices (no matter if the dominant new resources are solar or nuclear). Resulting sectoral and regional socio-economic dislocations are thus inevitable and can be deep and long-lasting (think of the economically depressed former major coal-mining regions), the necessary infrastructural trans-formations will be costly (valued in trillions of dollars) and inevitably protracted (requiring decades rather than years to put in place) and their diffusion will be uneven (they always have been: even in the US many rural areas were electrified only during the 1950s and some 2 billion people worldwide still have no electric lights!).

Beyond oil

A fundamental general consideration needs to be stressed before I proceed with a brief outline of alternatives to conventional liquid oil. Substitutions that are already technically proven (such as gas-to-liquid conversions) or that appear as highly promising future candidates (for example ethanol production from cellu-losic biomass) are nevertheless often seen as unacceptable or impractical simply because they cost (or are projected to cost) more than the conversion they are set to replace. This simplistic cost argument is misleading for three principal reasons. First, it does not acknowledge that the real cost of today's liquid fuels is higher (often substantially so) than the price directly paid by consumers. Second, it implies that only the resources and conversions secured with the lowest cost are worthy of consideration regardless of the environmental or strategic impli-cations of their use. Third, it ignores the fact that modern societies are already paying far less (as a share of disposable income) for their energy needs than at anytime in history and hence even a doubling of such vital expenditures would not be catastrophic.

The last point is true even in the country that is most addicted to excessive driving. Detailed surveys of US consumer spending show that in 2004 an average family spent less on gasoline (3.7% of all expenditure) than it did on home furnishing (3.8%) or on entertainment (5.1%). Why then should we be panicked by the prospect of an alternative motor fuel that retails (say, arbitrarily) at twice the price of today's gasoline? If that new fuel were to be used in vehicles operating with twice as high efficiency as today's cars (given the poor average performance of US cars this is an easily achievable goal) then even this low share of expenditure may remain unchanged! And the argument about unacceptably higher costs of alternative fuels is insufficient if they could be produced and converted with lower environmental burdens (including lower emissions of greenhouse gases) or if they will provide important strategic benefits.

Such considerations may drive future efforts to extract even more oil from known reservoirs: after all, even today's best enhanced recovery methods still leave behind 40–50% of the oil originally in place, and higher prices may justify more expensive recovery techniques. Mining of progressively poorer mineral ores is perhaps the best analogy. And beyond the conventional liquid oil there is much more oil that is harder to get, vast resources of nonconventional hydrocarbons whose recovery is already contributing to global supply and whose future inroads, depending on the changes in demand and on advances in technical innovation, may be slow and steady or widespread and relatively rapid. This continuum between conventional and non-conventional oil runs from medium heavy oils (25–18 °API, mobile at reservoir conditions) to extra heavy oils (20–7 °API, still somewhat mobile) to tar sands and bitumen (12–7 °API, non mobile) and finally to oil shales with no permeability.

Limited volumes of medium and of some extra heavy oils have been produced for many years in Saskatchewan and Venezuela. Alaska's North Slope also has large deposits of heavy oil: at least 20 and up to 40 Gb of this heavy oil are in place (as much as in Prudhoe and Kuparuk, the region's two supergiant conventional fields) but only a fifth of it is recoverable and the current production of viscous oil accounts for just 5% of the North Slope output and, obviously, the region's Arctic temperatures and permafrost make the oil extremely viscous and difficult to produce; a recovery technique that alternates water and gas injection seems to be the best choice. But most of the 4– 5 Tb of heavy oils in place are found in Venezuela's extra heavy oils (1.2 Tb, of which 270 Gb may be eventually recoverable) and in Alberta's tar sands (some 2.5 Tb of bitumen).

At the beginning of 2006 Canada's conventional oil reserves were about 5.6 Gb. The Canadian Association of Petroleum Producers adds to this 8.6 Gb of oil recoverable from the already developed commercial projects, and Alberta Energy and Utilities Board put the total of oil sands reserves that are now under active development at 174.4 Gb; this brought Canada's aggregate oil reserves to at least 180 Gb, compared to Saudi Arabia's 260 Gb. But Athabasca's ultimately recoverable oil may be eventually revalued to as much as 315 Gb, and that total would give Canada the world's largest oil reserves. By 2005 Alberta oil sands had yielded 1 Mbpd (with production costs of up to $25/b), Natural Resource Canada put the future oil production from Athabasca oil sands at 2 Mbpd by 2020, but the government of Alberta sees 3 Mbpd by 2020 and possibly 5 Mbpd in 2030.

The basic advantage of producing extra heavy oil in Venezuela's Orinoco Belt is that a high thermal gradient (reservoir temperature of 53°C) makes cold extraction possible. Annual output from several new projects developed with the participation of major international oil companies should be 600,000 bpd in 2008 at less than $7/b. Another Orinoco product is a boiler fuel (coal or gas substitute), a mixture of 70% natural bitumen, 30% water and a small amount of an additive

OIL FROM SANDS

Extraction of oil from oil sands was commercialized for the first time on a small scale during the late 1960s. Suncor was the first company to produce oil from Alberta oil sands near Fort McMurray in 1967, and the Syncrude consortium, formed in 1965, has been producing in the area since 1978. Both of these pioneering projects operate large oil sand mines, using huge excavators to mine the rock and the world's largest off-road trucks to transport it to a bitumen extraction plant from which it moves to an upgrading facility to yield light crude oil. Mining of Alberta oil sands, extraction of bitumen and its upgrading to light crude oil returns about six units of energy for every unit invested. Only about a fifth of all recoverable oil in Alberta's oil sands can be reached by surface mining, the rest will have to be extracted *in situ* and two techniques (see figure 28) have been commercialized so far, cyclic steam-stimulation (CSS) and steam-assisted gravity drainage (SAGD).

Imperial Oil's Cold Lake Project was the first CSS recovery that alternates periods of injecting hot pressurized steam (300°C, 11 MPa) into well bores with periods of soaking that loosens the bitumen. These cycles last from a few months to three years and the heated bitumen-water mixture is drawn from the same wells that were used for steam injection. On average, this process extracts about a quarter, and with follow-up processes up to 35%, of the bitumen originally present in sands. SAGD was patented by Imperial Oil in 1982 and EnCana Corporation is now its leading practitioner in Alberta oil sands. The process uses two horizontal wells (typically 500–800 m long) that are drilled near the bottom of an oil sands formation and are separated by a vertical distance of 5 m. Steam injected into the top well heats the surrounding bitumen that slowly drains into the bottom well from which it is lifted. The process recovers up to 60% of the oil but it has large water and energy needs (roughly one unit of energy as natural gas for steam generation is needed for every five units of heavy bitumen). EROEI (including the cost of extraction and delivery of the gas, and of oil upgrading) is no higher than three.

OIL FROM SANDS (*cont.*)

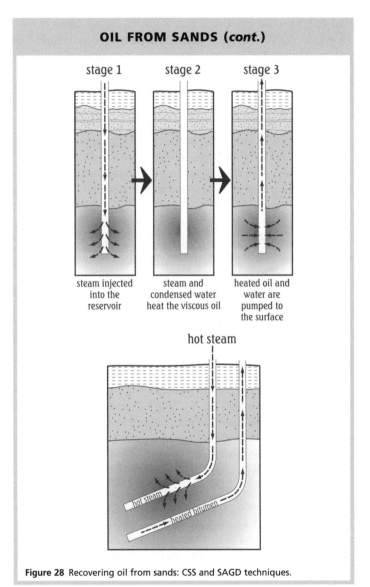

Figure 28 Recovering oil from sands: CSS and SAGD techniques.

that stabilizes the emulsion, that is sold as liquid *Orimulsión* by Petróleos de Venezuela. Future rates of non-conventional oil production (and its possible extension to vast oil shale resources, especially in the US and China) will be determined by a complex interplay of oil prices, perceptions of supply security and technical advances

Non-conventional oil will not be the only hydrocarbon resource that will add to the supply of conventional liquid fuels. The technical feasibility of gas-to-liquid conversion was demonstrated in 1923 with the production of motor fuels from coal gas by a process invented by Franz Fischer and Hans Tropsch in Germany. During WWII Fischer-Tropsch synthesis kept the Wehrmacht and Luftwaffe supplied with fuel, and since the 1950s South Africa's Sasol has used the process to reduce the country's dependence on fuel imports. The high capital costs of large Fischer-Tropsch plants have been a major deterrent to widespread commercialization but intensive research aimed at more efficient synthesis and smaller plant size has finally made this conversion a serious candidate for large-scale commercialization.

And displacement of oil by gas does not have to go through liquids. Direct substitution of liquids by natural gases has been underway for decades and it will continue for decades to come. As already noted, natural gas replaced fuel oil in heating all but a small share of homes both in North America and in Europe, and it has been substituted for fuel oil in many electricity-generating plants and in industrial enterprises. Natural gases are also highly valued petrochemical feedstocks. What is much less appreciated is that natural gas can replace motor gasoline in passenger cars with only minor engine modifications. Simply put, with the exception of flying and long-distance land and maritime transport (energy density of natural gas under normal pressure is only 1/1000 that of liquid fuel, making it unsuitable as a portable fuel sufficient for extended travel), everything that is done with liquid fuels can be done with gases.

NATURAL GASES: PROPERTIES AND RESERVES

Much like oils, natural gases are mixtures of variable proportions of hydrocarbons, but unlike oils they are primarily mixtures of just three of the simplest alkanes, methane, ethane and propane. Higher homologues (butane, pentane and hexane, are separated as natural gas liquids) and CO_2, H_2S, N, He, and water vapor, found in many gases, are also separated before the gases are compressed and transported by pipelines. Natural gases are commonly associated with crude oils but they also exist as free (dry) gases without any contact with crude oil in an oil reservoir or in entirely separate gas-bearing formations. Their heat content ranges between 30–45 MJ/m³ (35.5 MJ/m³ for CH_4), they are the least-polluting fossil fuels, and generate the least amount of CO_2 per unit of energy. As with crude oil, conventional gas reserves have been steadily increasing: they had nearly doubled between 1985 and 2005 when they stood at about 180 m³ or in energy terms nearly as much as the total reserves of conventional crude oil.

This increase has not only accommodated the expanding extraction (it grew by about 65% between 1985 and 2005, to 2.75 Tm³) but it lifted the global R/P ratio to sixty-seven years by 2005 (compared to fifty-six years in 1980 and to just over forty years in the early 1970s). Conventional reserves are concentrated in Russia (about 27% of the total), Iran (about 15%), Qatar (about 14%) and Saudi Arabia and the United Arab Emirates (4% each). The Middle East claims about 40% of the global total, much less than its share of crude oil. Gas associated with oil used to be simply flared as an unwanted by-product but this wasteful practice has declined with the rising demand for clean household and industrial fuel. In 1975 gas equal to about 14% of worldwide production was flared, with major sites visible on night-time satellite images as lights brighter than those of many large cities. By 2005 flaring was down to about 4% of global production, still equal to about half of Russia's (the world's largest) gas exports. Most of the flaring is now done in Nigeria, Iraq, Siberia, Iran and Algeria.

For decades those large natural gas reserves that could not be accessed by a pipeline could not be used, creating large stores of so called stranded gas. This limitation began to be addressed during the late 1950s and the early 1960s when the first lique-fied natural gas (LNG) tankers were used to export Algerian gas to the UK and France, and Indonesian gas to Japan. But the gas liquefaction plants and special tankers were expensive and the export remained limited. LNG occupies only about 1/600 the volume of natural gas but it must be cooled to -162°C and regasified after delivery. As both the liquefaction process and the construction of special tankers with highly insulated containers became more affordable LNG trade took off during the 1990s and its unfolding expansion will bring to market many gas resources that were previously considered completely stranded or uneconomical.

In 2005 there were twenty-nine liquefaction facilities in seventeen ports in Africa (Algeria, Libya, Egypt, Nigeria), the Middle East (Oman, Qatar, UAE), Asia (Brunei, Indonesia, Malaysia), Australia, Alaska and Trinidad and many more were under construction or in advanced stages of planning. Indonesia was the largest exporter (shipping to Japan, South Korea and Taiwan), followed by Malaysia (exporting to the same three East Asian countries), Qatar and Algeria (to the US, the EU and Turkey). In 2005 LNG tankers (now mostly with capacities in excess of 100,000 m^3) carried just over 25% of all traded natural gas to forty regasification sites in fifteen countries. Japan, South Korea, Spain, the US and Taiwan were the largest importers, soon to be joined by China.

Gas is thus finally becoming a truly global fuel but, as with crude oil, opinions about its future are divided. Not surprisingly, the advocates of an imminent oil peak see only a limited impact because they believe that the ultimate resources of natural gas are actually smaller than those of crude oil. But most geologists and resource economists envisage a gas-rich future, particularly once non-conventional gas resources begin to contribute more to the commercial recovery. As with crude oil, the latest US Geological Survey assessment of global natural gas resources indicates considerable prospects for further discoveries: it assumed 129 Tm^3 of remaining reserves, reserve growth in these known fields of 99 Tm^3, and undiscovered resources of 140 trillion m^3. With cumulative production of 47 Tm^3 this gives mean resources of about 415 trillion m^3, an equivalent of nearly 2.6 Tb of oil.

All of these figures refer to conventional resources only. The only non-conventional gas resource that is already exploited is coalbed methane. In the US potential resources of this gas would add about 15% to traditional sources. Similar volumes are present as shale gas and much larger resources are held in impermeable rocks in tight reservoirs. As large as these non-conventional resources may be they are all insignificant when compared to methane hydrates (clathrates) that were formed by the gas released from anoxic decomposition of organic sediments by methanogenic bacteria and are now trapped inside rigid lattice cages of frozen water molecules. Fully saturated gas hydrates have one CH_4 molecule for every 5.75 water molecules and hence one m^3 of hydrates contains as much as 164 m^3 of CH_4.

Hydrates can be found in polar continental sediments at depths between 150 m to 2.5 km and where the ocean bottom water is near 0°C hydrates are in aquatic sediments to depths of more than 1 km. The resource base of methane hydrates is so immense that only gross approximations are now possible: the US Geological Survey estimated that they can contain twice as much carbon as all other fossil fuels combined, and the volume of hydrates in US coastal waters may be as much as 1,000 times that of total conventional US gas reserves. Their commercial recovery faces many problems and it must also take into account the possibility of a sudden catastrophic release of some hydrate deposits into the atmosphere. But these challenges are hardly a valid argument for eliminating this enormous resource from future consideration as a major source of hydrocarbons (perhaps even by the middle of this century): doing so would be akin to the 1930 claim that any extraction of oil from offshore fields out of sight of land was impossible.

The combination of non-conventional oil, natural gas, and gas-to-liquid conversions means that hydrocarbons should be with us as major sources of global energy supply far beyond the middle of this century. In a speech accepting the Biennial OPEC Award for 2006 Peter Odell, one of the most astute, life-long, observers of the global oil scene, concluded that 'peak-oilers', much like their numerous predecessors, will soon be proven wrong, that the present contribution of oil and gas to the global energy supply will be only modestly reduced by 2050, that natural gas will surpass oil as the leading source, but that the oil industry will be, even in 2100, still larger than in 2000. And beyond this only slowly receding mixture of liquid and gaseous, conventional and non-conventional hydrocarbons are renewable energy flows.

Three of them will dominate any future efforts because of their inherently large magnitude: biomass fuels, wind, and direct solar radiation. Liquids from biomass (above all ethanol from sugar cane) are already displacing some gasoline, but the future should not belong to the currently heavily promoted (but in many ways problematic) conversion of grains (above all corn) to ethanol, but to innovative bioengineering processes converting more abundant cellulosic biomass, including crop residues and high-yielding perennial grasses planted on non-agricultural land. Commercial wind-powered electricity generation has already made major strides and in time even greater contributions will come from photovoltaic conversions. Although these conversions may seem to do little for expanding the supply of liquid fuels they could actually fit perfectly into a system of rechargeable hybrid cars.

The inherent fluctuations and unpredictability of photo-voltaic electricity generation in temperate latitudes would be much less of a problem for recharging plug-in hybrid cars than for lighting houses or running machines in a factory where electricity must be available on demand. In contrast, a car plugged in, in a garage or in a parking lot at a place of work would be recharged whenever a surge of renewable electricity became available. And, further in the future, once these conversions become much more economical, they would provide inexpensive electricity to produce hydrogen, the most energy-dense of all fuels and hence an excellent energy carrier in the post-fossil fuel world. However, George Olah, the Nobel Prize winner in chemistry for 1994, argues that a methanol, rather than hydrogen, economy would be the best choice. This liquid hydrocarbon (CH_3OH) can be prepared by a number of methods (above all by direct oxidative conversion of natural gas, and also by catalytic reduction of CO_2) and it is safer and less expensive to handle than hydrogen.

As with all long-range perspectives, it is counterproductive to pinpoint any rates of progress, dates or shares for these new energy conversions. In 2006 Sweden announced that it wants to be the first oil-free country by 2020 (and to do so without any reliance on nuclear generation), but given the inertia of massive and expensive energy infrastructures it is inevitable that oil and gas will remain the dominant primary energy sources of most modern nations for decades to come. This we know for certain: although a nation can switch from one dominant form of energy to another in a matter of years, energy transitions are normally protracted affairs, extending across decades rather than years. And neither the tempo nor the eventual achievements of these long transitions from first commercial uses to widespread embrace and to eventual domination can be judged by the state of affairs during the initial stages of expansion. Today's forecasts of contributions and performances of renewable energies may be akin (giving just a few of many possible examples) to predicting in 1950 the 2005 achievements in geophysical exploration, offshore oil drilling, electronic computing or intercontinental aviation.

Energy transitions – from biomass to coal, from coal to oil, from oil to natural gas, from direct use of fuels to electricity – have stimulated technical advances and driven our inventiveness. Inevitably, they bring enormous challenges for both producers and consumers, necessitate the scrapping or reorganization of extensive infrastructures, are costly and protracted and cause major socio-economic dislocations. But they have created more productive and richer economies, and modern societies will not collapse just because we face yet another of these grand transformations. The world beyond oil is still many decades away but we should see the path toward that era as one of very challenging, but also immensely rewarding, opportunities as modern civilization severs its dependence on fossil carbon.

Appendix A: Units, abbreviations and their definitions and conversions

barrel	b	unit of volume	42 gallons; 158.98 L
centi	c	multiplier prefix	10^{-2}
cubic meter	m³	unit of volume	1000 L; 264.17 gal
dead weight ton	dwt	unit of capacity	1.016 t
foot	ft	unit of length	0.3 m
gallon	(US) gal	unit of volume	3.785 L
giga	G	multiplier prefix	10^9
gram	g	unit of mass	
inch	in	unit of length	2.5 cm
joule	J	unit of energy	
kilo	k	multiplier prefix	10^3
kilogram	kg	unit of mass	1000 g
kilometer	km	unit of length	1000 m
liter	L	unit of volume	1000 mL³; 0.001 m³
mega	M	multiplier prefix	10^6
meter	m	unit of length	100 cm; 3.28 ft
milli	m	multiplier prefix	10^{-3}
pascal	Pa	unit of pressure	
tera	T	multiplier prefix	10^{12}
ton (metric)	t	unit of mass	1000 kg

Appendix B: Additional reading and websites

Books

Ahlbrandt, T.S. et al. 2005. *Global Resource Estimates from Total Petroleum Systems*. Tulsa, OK: American Association of Petroleum Geologists.

Brantly, J.E. 1971. *History of Oil Well Drilling*. Houston, TX: Gulf Publishing.

Campbell, C.J. 2005. *Oil Crisis*. Brentwood: Multi-Science Publishing.

Cordesman, A.H. and K.R. al-Rodhan. 2006. *The Global Oil Market: Risks and Uncertainties*. Washington, DC: CSIS Press.

Deffeyes, K.S. 2001. *Hubbert's Peak: The Impending World Oil Shortage*. Princeton, NJ: Princeton University Press.

Marcel, V. 2006. *Oil Titans: National Oil Companies in the Middle East*. London: Chatham House.

Maugeri, L. 2006. *The Age of Oil: The Mythology, History, and Future of the World's Most Controversial Resource*. Westport, CT: Praeger Publishers.

National Energy Board. 2006. *Canada's Oil Sands: Opportunities and Challenges to 2015*. Ottawa: NEB.

Odell, P. R. 2004. *Why Carbon Fuels Will Dominate the 21st Century's Global Energy Economy*. Brentwood: Multi-Science Publishing.

Olah, G.A., A. Goeppert and G.K.S. Prakash. 2006. *Beyond Oil and Gas: The Methanol Economy*. Weinheim: Wiley-VCH.

Selley, R.C. 1997. *Elements of Petroleum Geology*. San Diego, CA: Academic Press.

Smil, V. 2007. *Energy in Nature and Society: General Energetics of Complex Systems*. Cambridge, MA: The MIT Press.

Websites

American Association of Petroleum Geologists: www.aapg.org

American Petroleum Institute: www.api.org

British Petroleum: www.bp.com

British Petroleum Statistical Review of World Energy: www.bp.com

Canadian Association of Petroleum Producers: www.capp.ca

Chevron Corporation: www.chevron.com

Exxon Mobil: www.exxonmobil.com

OPEC: www.opec.org

Platts Oil: www.platts.com

Royal Dutch Shell: www.shell.com

Saudi Aramco: www.saudiaramco.com

Schlumberger: www.slb.com

Schlumberger Oilfield Glossary: www.glossary.oilfield.slb.com

US Energy Information Administration, international statistics: www.eia.doe.gov

World Oil: www.worldoil.com

Index